# The Forgotten Friend

*A simple guide to a new way of being with YOU*

Janice Fuchs, LCSW

# *Dedication*

*This book is dedicated to my beautiful daughters Emma and Noelle, who have been my greatest inspiration. I love you both dearly and may you always know the friendship within.*

# Acknowledgments

This book is complete because of the help and support of some wonderful people to whom I am deeply grateful.

First I wish to thank Abby Leefer, my best friend and inspiration for: how you should treat yourself like your best friend would. Thanks for encouraging me to finish this book, without your support it would still be sitting on my computer. Thank you for all your editorial help and for always knowing exactly what I was trying to say.

I wish to thank Karen Valadez for being the best life coach and friend; you have been such a gift in my life.

I wish to thank Loraine Page, an earth angel who just appeared and out of the kindness of her heart took on the task of editing my book with such love and care.

Lastly, I wish to give special thanks and gratitude to my Fiancé, Brian Glidden for your love, endless support and a lot of patience with this whole process. Thank you for all your help in all the many ways you have contributed.

# Contents

# Preface

## *The clock*

I have 45 minutes once a week. During this short time I do my best to inspire, convince, and sometimes plead with my clients to consider developing a loving relationship--a friendship--with themselves. The time ticks away and I keep my intention on what I want to teach. I talk with compassion and without judgment or anger. I accept and listen to the story of their feelings. I choose to focus on the positive and let anything negative go. I listen in a way that enables me to hear and see my clients fully.

My client's true nature always emerges and I can see the perfection in them even among their flaws. It is a similar feeling to the one I have with my children. In sessions, my self-interest fades and their happiness becomes mine. I feel being a psychotherapist is a very spiritual profession. I would never have anticipated that their well-being would be as important to me as my own. I see and feel the oneness between us in those moments and I often feel the presence of a higher power. They let me see them at their most vulnerable and in their darkest moments of despair. I hold a light for them during these times.

The words I hear play over in my mind and in my heart: "Teach them how to love themselves more. Teach them to remember who they really are in all their perfection. Teach them love, for that is what we all are and where we all came from." I wish I could capture and express how I feel in those moments of oneness.

The voice, the whisper I hear during my sessions, is the same voice I hear while meditating and the same voice that has inspired me to take my mission of helping to a larger audience.

This voice, this inner knowing, this connection became apparent to me as I saw the importance of developing a loving relationship with myself. When I took the time to really listen to myself and open up to my heart and soul, I discovered parts of myself, and a connection to God, source, and love, that have always been with me but I never knew existed. We have the tendency to look outside ourselves for just about everything--happiness, wisdom, support – when we have "all" within us every moment of our lives.

I believe we are a part of God-source-love and when we develop an inner relationship filled with love and compassion, it then is only natural that God would be found in these feelings, moments, and loving actions. Once we find God within, that is when things really begin to get good.

# The Golden Rule

We all know the Golden Rule: "Do unto others as you would want done unto you." The Golden Rule is a beautiful reminder of how we should treat others. It's a way for us to put ourselves in someone else's place to see how we would like to be treated, and then extend that treatment to another. It helps us to stay on the right path, the path of kindness, compassion, and fairness.

I believe there is another way to use this rule. Even before offering that gift to others, I believe we need to reverse it and use it within ourselves. I believe we should be treating ourselves the way that we would treat our most beloved friend. We could be giving ourselves the same support, consideration, gentleness, and understanding we give to those we love. This reversal is a new way to help us approach the relationship we create with ourselves. The friendship, this new way of being with us, is worth looking at for our own happiness sake. It's a path, a path of mindfulness of how to treat us first before we attend to the needs of others.

Why? What's at stake? It is the quality of your entire life. It's like having either the most supportive, loving friend with you walking by your side in life--or an enemy. This is a critical choice in life because a friend has the power to support you in your deepest desires and dreams, while an enemy sabotages your every move. It's the difference between true happiness and fulfillment or a life of pain, fear, and insecurity. In this book I will help guide you along this path, and as my life and the lives of many others have drastically changed, yours will too. I hope you take this short but valuable journey with me!

# In the beginning

I have found with my clients and in my own life that we often treat others better than we treat ourselves. Think about it: Others treat you really well, but then you go home and treat yourself badly. Where is the good in that?

People can be told how wonderful they are, but if they don't see their own value and the value in treating themselves well, they still suffer. Using the Golden Rule on yourself improves the relationship you have within you, and then impacts the quality and success of your life.

For the longest time I didn't realize a great source of my unhappiness stemmed from this inner relationship. When I began mindfully treating myself better and started to develop a loving relationship with myself, my life improved beyond what I thought possible. When I began to share this idea with my clients, the idea of them developing a loving relationship with themselves, the response I often heard was: Love myself? Really? I don't even really like me!

I understand their reaction and have felt the same way at different points in my own life. The next question, after the shock of what I just said wears off, is: If this is going to make my life better, then how do I even begin to do this "loving myself" business? This is the beginning of our work together. When my clients become mindful and practice these ideas, their lives improve right before my eyes.

I decided to share this work because I know for the majority of people, psychotherapy is not an option, either because of a time issue, money, or just a fear of the unknown. I think we have come a long way in our views of seeking therapy, but many of my clients still feel there is a stigma attached and feel uneasy about telling people they come.

My intention and deepest desire is to help as many people as I can to feel better in their lives and live the life they were meant to. I am passionate about helping people find their own true passion and life purpose, and I have found the only way to get there is through developing the best relationship with yourself that is humanly possible. We all have "the forgotten friend" within us and the power in developing this friendship is truly life changing. I hope you will give yourself this gift and continue reading and find this friendship within you!

# Developing a loving friendship with yourself

Why is it a good idea to focus your attention on developing a good, loving friendship with yourself?

What are the benefits?

I can name many. After working as a psychotherapist for over twenty years, I have begun to understand that our happiness really comes down to how we treat ourselves.

From this relationship with ourselves stems our mood, good or bad. How we talk to and treat ourselves daily impacts us on so many levels. It impacts our self-image, relationships, work, parenting, and decisions. When you shift your focus from the outside world to your inside world, you will start to see what you have been doing to yourself.

Most of my clients express some form of criticism about themselves within the first five minutes of session. As I began developing a better relationship with myself, I became so sensitive to the awful things people are silently saying to themselves all day long.

My heart breaks when I hear people of all ages speak to themselves and about themselves in this way. But I really didn't understand it until I noticed it happening within me. How sad I felt for myself when I realized I was telling myself I was a horrible person. And for what? Not being perfect? Not being "good enough"? I found endless reasons to put myself down. Funny, I realized I never did this with my clients, only to myself and sometimes to the people closest to me. To most people I was endlessly compassionate, understanding, and supportive. To me? Not so much.

# Fall in love

What I began to realize is so many of us need to change our focus off loving others, and onto loving ourselves. Is this selfish? No, simply because you will start to feel better. You become happier, your mood improves, and your relationships improve. Life becomes safe and you feel more grounded and loved. And this feeling will extend out to everyone around you.

Think of how you feel when you fall in love with another person. Feels good doesn't it? Now imagine if you felt that way within yourself. Since you never leave yourself, and you must be with yourself 24 hours a day, guess who has the greatest impact on you?

YOU... . Just think about this for one moment. Even as I write this, my commitment fears start to creep up and that thought can make me feel a little suffocated. But how true it is! We are with ourselves for our whole lives, every second, hour, day, week, forever. We are our own biggest commitment. The power that lies in that simple fact blows me away. So, I will no longer blame my parents, my horrible boyfriends, or ex-husband for the state of my well being. Guess what? I won't even blame myself, because if I had realized the importance of developing self-love years ago, my life could have been very different.

Sadly, we are not taught this and I think now is the time to start learning how to love ourselves better. We are taught that everything outside us will make us happy, and it does for a moment, and then that moment passes. But what are you doing in between all those great heady, high moments when you are alone with you? How are you treating yourself?

# Stop the insanity today

Isn't it a good idea to make this inner relationship your first priority?

I can say when I set the intention daily to have a positive, non-abusive relationship with myself, I just plain old feel better. My day goes smoothly, the world seems safe, and I can relax and take a deep breath.

Where do you start? How do you do this? It's simple: You start with the intention and commitment to treat yourself in a good and loving manner ALL the time--especially when you don't even like you. We take a vow when we get married, why not take one to ourselves?

I promise to love, honor, and cherish myself for all the days of my life. I promise to always listen to my feelings, to be my biggest fan, my greatest cheerleader in life. I promise to never abandon myself and to keep myself safe. When we can do this within ourselves, then getting married is a piece of cake because you have already been in your greatest relationship and you are taking it with you. You have met the love of your life and it's you. I am worth that and so are you.

It doesn't have to mean you are perfect. It means at any given moment you do the best thing for yourself that you are capable of doing. So, whether it's eating ice cream or taking a walk or a nap, you can ask yourself: What do I really need right now? Let me just give it to myself, no one is watching over my shoulder. I don't have to be so hard on myself or so perfect.

I believe even God wants us to be happy and safe. He doesn't care how much we weigh or what kind of car we drive. He wants you and me to be happy to find him within us. I believe we are all a part of God and when we love ourselves we connect with him. When we are attacking ourselves, he doesn't judge it or get mad, he just waits for us to choose him again.

So take your vow when you are in a low point and see no redeeming qualities in yourself. When you are in self-attack mode, remember what you promised to do.

# Listen closely feelings tell a story

Listen to each of your feelings when you are upset or scared. Each feeling can tell us a story if we take the time to listen to it.

We tend to wait for other people to listen and validate our feelings, and that feels so good when it happens. But I have found that many times people are either not available or it's hard for them to validate what we feel because of their own feelings. Feelings are so personal to us, so unique and special. We sometimes have a hard time understanding why others feel the way they do. We have little practice in accepting feelings as they are – instead we tend to judge ourselves and others. We have so little acceptance and understanding that feelings aren't right or wrong, they just are.

I recommend that you share and validate your feelings with yourself first, and then the need to have others understand them becomes less important and much less frustrating. You need to understand and accept your own feelings, and still try to like yourself. I spend a lot of time in therapy with people just feeding back who they really are to them. It's as if they have no idea who they really are, all their strengths and weaknesses. I try to help them see themselves accurately, to accept themselves, and to see that it's in their best interest to like and even learn to love themselves. When they can do that, they no longer need me.

If we can love other people with their imperfections, why not ourselves?

You need to learn how to "get" YOU, to understand and accept yourself, and most importantly, to try to treat yourself lovingly and with kindness.

Just remember when you are getting to know yourself and your feelings, be gentle with yourself! Make it safe, because the only way you will be able to openly admit your feelings to yourself is if you commit to accepting and not judging them.

If you judge your feelings then you will shut yourself down just like you would in any other relationship. If you went to a friend, took a risk and opened up and shared how scared you were about something, and they said "That's stupid!" or "Why do you feel that way?", you would close up shop and go home. Your relationship with yourself is no different!

When I start to judge or criticize myself, I will turn away from wanting to listen to my own feelings because the judgment is too uncomfortable. This is why you have to vow to accept every feeling you have. Listen with no judgment, only acceptance and love.

# A safe accepting home inside you

I accept every feeling I have with love and I listen to the story behind each one. I am that important, and all my feelings, even if they don't make sense, are very important and want my attention.

When you create this safe place then there is no need to push your feelings away or down.

Feelings are a very important part of us, yet often we treat them like our worst enemy. We are better with accepting our good feelings because they feel good. But our bad, scary, fearful feelings get left behind. We will do anything to avoid those. We pretend we don't have them; we push them down with food, alcohol, or drugs. We are very clever in how we have managed to hide them even from ourselves.

That's okay and understandable, because we have so little understanding and training in how to cope with them. But when you make your inner "you" a very safe and accepting home, you can stop hiding and face these uncomfortable feelings.

I have also noticed that even the good feelings we have we sometimes want to avoid as well. Good feelings can bring up our fears of loss. What if this good feeling doesn't last? Sometimes we feel guilty for feeling good when others are suffering. If we can just develop a different approach to our feelings, it can be easier to listen, accept, and enjoy the good ones fully, and be our very best friend when our deepest most painful feelings emerge.

In my approach, I try to say to myself that my feelings are telling me about my experience in this world. They are an integral part of me, a very special part, the sensitive part that demonstrates my perspective. In showing me how I am experiencing this world, they are never wrong. However, I have to accept that they belong only to me and my experience, and no one in this world shares these identical experiences and feelings. It is the reason people sometimes have a hard time understanding where I am coming from. The good news is that if I give my feelings my time, attention and acceptance, they will always begin to make sense to me.

Our feelings are just another experience we have in our bodies. They don't define us, and they don't make us good or bad. This inner emotional world is just as important as our outer world, maybe even more important. Our feelings are our ongoing barometer of how we experience our world and how it affects us, from the day we are born to the day we die. Learning to understand and support all your feelings is one of the greatest gifts and experiences you can give yourself. When you love someone you try very hard to understand

and support his or her feelings. We could do this with ourselves as well.

# Story of feelings

Here is an example of the "story of feelings" with a client of mine who I will call Mary.

Mary came in for a session feeling very upset that her good friend didn't do anything special for her son's birthday. Mary, a very thoughtful and caring mom in her twenties, had always given a special cake or a present when her friend's son had a birthday. But when it came to Mary's son, her friend never reciprocated. Anyone could relate to this and understand being upset, but Mary was very angry and hurt and was having trouble getting over this issue. I could see it clearly because I have been working with Mary for a long time, so I know the back story that was fueling these feelings.

Mary's mom was very self-centered, and never really went out of her way for Mary. In many ways, Mary was the mother to her mom while growing up and even today. I believe on some level Mary vowed she would never treat people the way her mom had treated her. Because of this Mary always put other people first, always doing thoughtful things for them, such as buying nice birthday presents, babysitting their children, and on and on. She was very thoughtful and helpful, and was there for everyone--except herself. Mary unconsciously was drawn to people who shared similar traits to her mom.

It's as if we have an internal magnet to people who are like our family. We are drawn to them and they are drawn to us. We are sensitive to certain traits in people and it's often those very traits that trigger our wounds. There are psychological theories that posit that we are unconsciously drawn to people just like our family because we are trying to work through and heal those primary relationships, and that may be partly true. But clients also have people in their life who are nothing like their family and they still will be sensitive to the traits they have wounds around.

My conclusion is that it is probably both: We are attracted to people who share traits of our family because they feel like home to us. Yet other people who seem so different still stumble upon our "wounds" and then there we are again, hurt, angry, confused, and disillusioned. Since we all share common feelings and needs, how could we not at some point trigger each other's childhood wounds? The most important thing, however, is to know what to do, how to treat ourselves when this happens.

To get back to Mary: In this experience with her friend, she was feeling hurt by the same trait her mom had – apparent self-centeredness. This hurt and frustration burst into my office with Mary. I got the "story" of her feelings. She was feeling that same hurt she felt with her mom when her mom didn't think of her or buy her the special birthday present. So when this was happening to her son she was outraged and very angry. She was reliving her own childhood hurt and disappointment.

This was the "story" of Mary's feelings. It would be helpful if she could see that the majority of her pain was old. It was 75 percent old, 25 percent new. It's not that she wasn't justified in being hurt by her friend's thoughtlessness; it's just not the whole story.

On one level we know this. We feel it to be true when we say we are overreacting. But we don't take the time to listen to and acknowledge our own feelings and the story behind them. Instead, we chastise ourselves for being upset. When we do accept and explore our feelings, they make total sense and we can begin to bring ourselves back from the time warp of our past pain into our current lives. This is an act of love on our part – to take our time to trace our stories, their beginning, middle, and end. We can do this to make sense to ourselves, and to feel better. Sounds difficult, but over time you begin to see the same issues being triggered by many people in your life. I tell my clients that sometimes our feelings cause us to grab our past pain and hurt – from the old childhood bag. We don't fully realize it's an old bag but we can put it away once we realize we went back there. When we can do this, the 25 percent of pain is much more manageable.

Since we usually turn outward to deal with our feelings, turning back inward takes a little mindfulness on our part. The benefit of turning toward ourselves and taking responsibility for all our feelings is that it gives us back our power, and the ability to understand and move on. When we go outward with our feelings and blame others we can't soothe them properly. We get stuck in them like quicksand. If we allow ourselves to experience our feelings fully, to know they are 75 percent about us and our experiences, we can accept them and begin to move forward.

Mary can say to herself, I am thoughtful and loving, and I am worthy despite what my mom did or anyone else does. I will spoil myself with love, attention, and presents, and when my friends set off this feeling again I might remember the story behind it and know exactly what my next step will be.

It doesn't mean Mary has to give up being kind and thoughtful to others. It gives Mary the perspective that some people are like her, and she will get that back from them, and that others are not. Mary doesn't need to change anything about herself. She just has to remind herself when this wound is triggered that she can listen to the story and choose not to beat herself and her friend up over it, but instead give herself what she needs.

# Affirmation time

I will unconditionally love and accept myself.

Before I started this relationship-friendship with myself, this affirmation was just words that I was repeating. Honestly, it didn't help, because until I started to try and treat myself better, I didn't see how little love and acceptance I had for myself. So as you do this, don't freak out when you begin to see how crappy you have been to yourself. Now, this affirmation has come alive for me and I totally get what this simple statement means. It is so much more than words.

Often we treat ourselves as slave drivers: the house must be clean, my children need to get A's, I have to work full time, and make a lot of money. I need to take vacations. I have to be nice and supportive to everyone around me, and on and on.

As I take my supportive self with me and drop the mean one, everything I do becomes easier. If something doesn't get done, I don't go into self-attack. I go into self-love, or try to. I begin to look at all the things I did get accomplished and acknowledge what a great job I did today. I remind myself of the bigger picture: my own well-being.

Here are some questions I ask myself on a daily basis. Maybe you can begin to use some of them:

Did I treat myself well today? Was I able to stop long enough to eat lunch? Did I laugh? Did I have fun today? Sometimes I get so serious I have to remind myself, "Hey, what happened to that fun teenager who used to crack everyone up? Where did she go?" Well, when I treat myself better I find her in the closet with all my old pictures and albums! I dust her off and she comes back to life. What type of atmosphere are you creating inside you – and as a result outside you? Take a good day and really put it under a microscope: What's going on with you on those days?

Are you saying nicer things to yourself? Are the people around you feeding back nice things to you? Is the sun shining? What makes your day? Is it getting praise from your boss? It can be a smile or someone letting you go ahead when you can't make that left turn, and the person in the other car has compassion for you and lets you go through. What creates your best day? Sometimes you just wake up feeling good and that feeling carries over. Whatever it is for you, I challenge you to believe you can give those things to yourself more often.

When you are struggling with a painful situation, here are some questions that are helpful to ask yourself: Can I say that to myself in a kinder way? Where am I being too hard on myself? What's my tone with me – is it sarcastic? Is it hostile?

Sometimes it is easier to see and hear the tone you are taking with yourself if you look at how you are talking to your spouse and kids. Sometimes you can catch it with your friends, but usually people are the nicest to friends and strangers. I can get a snapshot of how I am talking to myself on any particular day through observing my interactions with my spouse and kids. Are the words that leave my mouth tense and stressful? Do they have a sarcastic tone? Am I fooling around and joking with my kids? Am I creating a happy, fun home – or a boring, dull and work-driven or critical home? All of these things are usually a reflection of how we are treating ourselves, and of our internal dialogue and expectations.

Having more acceptances for who you are today can help you to begin to change to a more loving version of you, a happier you. Since I found my teenager inside me, I don't ever want to lose her again. I take her out, we laugh and watch TV and eat "bad" (yummy) foods if we feel like it.

When I share her with my kids we have really fun nights, and they look at me like "Wow, I like this mom – where has she been?" Well, she was a little stressed, believing that all the things she had to get done were more important than paying attention to her well being. Even as I have been writing this, I notice the wash piling up and I have a thousand things to do, but instead of beating myself up over it I remind myself I am doing something really important. The laundry will always be there waiting to be done, but now I can put my happiness before it.

Teaching and creating is like breathing for me, and when I do it I feel so happy and satisfied. Until I developed this new relationship with myself I couldn't write one word without my inner critic pouncing on me, looking over my shoulder and judging every word not good enough. I have replaced this critic with support and love. That simple change in how I treat myself has made a world of difference, and it can for you, too. Become super supportive of all your ideas. They are as individual as you are. What I want and like to do is very different than you, but we can value these differences. Value yourself, support yourself, and encourage yourself.

# Unconditional love

Unconditionally loving yourself is a tremendously worthwhile practice, and it is part of any good friendship. Through unconditional love you learn to let go, be happy, to enjoy your life and the moment you are living in. Over time and with practice, developing this loving relationship-friendship will help soften you and raise you above the demands you place on yourself. The process of creating your life is intermingled with your love for yourself, and the practice of unconditional self-love ensures that you will love yourself enough to stay on your right path.

As I am writing this I just heard the news that Philip Seymour Hoffman, a wonderful and talented actor, died of a drug overdose at 46 – too young. I think, as many do, how could this happen? He had it all; a wonderful career, tons of money, an exciting life. I think that if I had that life, I would be happy. Then I see my own life and see how others may also view it as a happy, successful life.

Before I started practicing this new type of relationship with myself, I could just as easily have fallen into drugs to medicate the pain of my "shoulds." I like many fall prey to "should thinking." How I should be thinner, I should be making more money, I should be traveling more, I should eat better, I should be exercising. I should be a vegetarian. I should be a better parent. I should be a better cook. Pearl Fritz, founder of Gestalt therapy would tell his clients to stop "shoulding" all over you! I agree! Even though it's a funny way to say it, doing this to us is terribly damaging, and I want to help people stop.

We all know that loving ourselves is a key ingredient to a happy life, but my clients often look to me and say but HOW? How do I love myself when most of the time I don't even LIKE myself?

My answer to them is practice. We are given the chance to love and forgive ourselves daily. Every time we make a mistake or do something imperfect it's our opportunity to treat ourselves with either love or condemnation. The choice is ours, and I am always encouraging my clients and myself to choose again! Choose to treat yourself with the compassion of the most loving parent you can imagine. Would they be mad at you for not keeping your house clean enough? Choose a Spiritual master or an Archangel – would they talk to you the way you talk to yourself? Somehow it is easier to imagine the loving words that God, Jesus, or Archangel Michael would speak to me, and I choose those words to speak to myself now.

# Keep the focus on you

Love yourself enough to keep the focus on you. I joke around with my clients all the time about how impossible it is to control another person. You can barely control yourself, and you think you can control others!! No way.

Isn't this true? Think of the last time someone tried to control you. How did that feel? How did you react? Yet somehow we think we know what's best for others. Where we get this idea is beyond me, but it's what we do, so naturally. Being a therapist, I actually got a license to tell people what to do, or so I thought. I quickly found out it doesn't work.

Therapy is more about creating a space for people to safely explore their lives, their feelings, and beliefs. What I try to do is to give my clients that safe space, and also some education and tools. But it is totally up to them to implement them. Education and awareness and unconditional love can sometimes bring about change for people. But, as with the ideas presented in this book, it's up to you to try them.

I believe it really benefits us when we give up trying to control people and situations, when we stop getting lost in our relationships with our spouses, our children, and our friends. We have to be really careful to not let ourselves do that. Because as we attend to their life, we are distracted from the work we are meant to do on ourselves. Getting stuck is a red flag, and we can get stuck in other people's lives and in our own.

In our own life, we can get stuck in our mind, in our thoughts, and in our feelings. When someone triggers us, when someone says or does something that hurts us, we get angry, hurt, and confused – and we can get stuck and lost. We can spend a lot of time in these triggered states. Some people are very anxious about their kids or about their finances. Maybe their relationship is always a concern. Maybe all three! Our mind bounces around from one to another, thinking how can I fix this? There is always a theme and a state of mind that we fall into and get stuck on.

My client Lisa, a professional photographer, can't understand why her parents are so insensitive to her. She feels they are very critical and at times mean. She gets "stuck" by taking it personally, which is so easy to do. But I can see how that takes her totally away from her own life and purpose. It's like we get OCD around certain things, and we are like a dog with a bone – it feels impossible to drop the thing that is occupying your mind. Some people bounce between multiple themes. Whatever these obsessive states center on for you, you can probably agree it is extremely tiring and time consuming!

What's your theme? What do you spend most of your time thinking about and worrying about? Is it weight, exercise, money, your relationships, kids, or your health? Maybe it is one or all of the above. Generally, most people have one or two that consistently distress and consume them.

I encourage myself, and my clients, to love ourselves enough to work on letting go of trying to control these triggers as quickly as possible. They are detours off your path and these detours can take you all over before you can get back on the highway.

So, when you have to take a detour, as we all do sometimes, listen to your feelings with patience, love, and compassion, and try to keep the focus on you. Try to resist the temptation to put it outside yourself.

Going back to my client Lisa, with the critical parents, I say to her, "Don't focus on your parents, on trying to figure out why they keep treating you this way. Keep it on you. Don't take them personally, they are just doing to you what they do to themselves and what was done to them. So, nurture yourself through this pain and then do something nice for you. Let them go. They can't change, and this focus on how they treat you is hurting you so much."

This is a hard process, and it has derailed her from moving on with her own life so often. So, I keep encouraging her to try. The pain in this relationship keeps her obsessed and stuck on trying to fix it or undo it. I do understand. It's hard to stop focusing on what hurts you. It can feel like it has a vise grip hold on us, but obsessing about it really doesn't help or change anything.

Today if something has you obsessed you might ask yourself, if I wasn't thinking or worrying about this situation, what else would I be doing? This question can help un-stick you, get you off the detour and back onto the highway of creating your day. This is really where developing a loving relationship-friendship with you becomes so important.

Whatever is triggering you, eating at you, keeping you stuck and upset, the next step is to help yourself out of it with love, compassion, and kindness. Instead, we usually blame or berate others or ourselves! Just think how it would feel if you were to speak to yourself with the voice of a supportive loving friend. If someone you love makes a mistake, acts in an imperfect way, or is hurt by someone, do you blame and chastise them? Probably not! If every time you are upset or obsessed you react to yourself with love and kindness, you will get out of those feelings much more quickly.

# Put down the snow globe

While I was meditating the other day, a practice I enjoy to relax and connect spiritually, I saw an image of a snow globe. I thought about how many times I have used the snow globe metaphor when talking with my clients. I tell my clients, "Look, our whole world can get shaken up and turned upside down just like when we shake this snow globe."

It can be a trigger like an argument with your boyfriend or a problem at work. Whatever the cause, our inner feeling state can be shaken up and it feels very disorienting. It causes us not to see clearly and things become confusing and cloudy just like in the globe.

In time, just like with a snow globe, we can see the snow settling and the landscape emerging once again. Our feelings, our inner states, are like the shaken snow, so all we have to do is, with patience and love, wait and watch the snow fall gently to the ground.

How many times does your snow globe get shaken each day? How many times are you the one shaking it? We can see how often we are responsible for disrupting our inner emotional home. There are times when it's an outside source but many times we are the ones with our hands on the globe. I have had the experience myself of picking up my snow globe, then putting it down, then picking it up over and over around a difficult issue. I can walk around feeling very shaken for most of my day. When I am having trouble letting something go, now I think of this snow globe analogy, and encourage myself to put the globe down.

What can we do when this happens and we are shaken up? Watch the snow fall, let it settle. We can watch our feelings in a non-judgmental way. When we do this for ourselves we can see the snow does settle, just as our feelings do when we accept, understand, and release them. Things become clear again and we are back on our path.

We deserve to have longer periods of peace within ourselves, so that we have time to do all the things we need and love to do – with our happy company. We don't want to live in a shaken globe. The mess makes us moody and unproductive, and that's not living our best life.

When someone picks up your globe and shakes it, it's not about you. It's that other person's decision to shake it and we don't have to take that action personally. I know it feels so personal, and they did, after all, metaphorically speaking, pick up my snow globe – so how could it not be about me?

It's not an easy thing to understand or believe but most attacks come from people attacking themselves first. When we are feeling loving and our lives are feeling pretty good at the moment, then the odds of you or me picking up someone's globe is highly unlikely.

But if you woke up and your car has a flat, you are late for work, and your boss is mad at you, I bet you are at high risk for grabbing not only your snow globe but possibly five others as the day goes on! We just displace our own feelings in trying to manage our internal pain. It feels justified at times, but it really never is, it's just a projection. When we do shake someone else's globe, later we often feel guilty and try to justify our behavior. Somewhere inside, we usually know it was an overreaction, our own reaction to something else that has been bothering us.

We all have had those moments when things are just not right within us and then we start with everyone around us. It's a normal reaction to life. It just helps to be aware of this so that we can have more compassion for others and ourselves, and not take it so personally when they do it to us.

I notice some people work very hard not to shake others' globes, but they shake their own most of the time. On the occasion they do shake others' globes, it's hard for them to see. And they get very upset when others shake theirs, because they work so hard not to do it to anyone.

Some people shake others most of the time, and rarely their own. Then there are people that do both equally. Depending on your pattern, it's either harder or easier for you to see this behavior. But it's worth understanding and accepting because it can help to reduce your own guilt or not take other people's actions so personally.

My client Pete, a stocky accountant, came into session very angry over his son smoking pot, and in the house no less. Understandably, this is an issue that has to be dealt with. By smoking pot, his son grabbed Pete's globe and gave it a good shake. As we talked, he began blaming himself. He had addictions on his side of the family and he felt this was the reason his son was now addicted to pot. Now the snow globe was in his hand and he was shaking it himself in self-attack.

I explained to him that I don't see it that way and why. At this point, I am trying to get him to voluntarily give me his snow globe so I can put it down for him. In time, he does and we process the situation. I explain the nature of addictions and we come up with a game plan for him to deal with his son. By the end of the session I am able to hand him back his snow globe hoping he will take good care of it!

There is no guarantee that Pete won't shake it as soon as leaves. But he still has the ability to talk differently to himself even if he can't put his snow globe down. We don't have to let anything rattle or shake us. But when it happens – and it always does – we can look at our globe and patiently and lovingly wait for our feelings to settle as the snow falls to the ground. With practice and a deep love for ourselves we can work on keeping our inner home quiet and peaceful.

If you have a snow globe, keep it by your bedside as a reminder of how much control you have over your inner environment... and how peaceful a scene it can be.

# Stop the rejection

Acceptance means acceptance of all you are: what you look like, how much you weigh, what you do for a living, how you think, what you feel. Everything. The good and not-so-good parts. It means learning and accepting that even what you have deemed unacceptable about yourself is okay. For ourselves, we often have very little tolerance and have a slave driver mentality. The house must be clean, my children need to get do well in school, I have to work full time, and make a lot of money. I need to take vacations. I have to be nice and supportive to everyone around me, and on and on.

We can be like little pressure cookers waiting to explode. It's become hard for us to cut everyone and ourselves a little slack. It's okay if the house inside and outside isn't perfect! Sometimes I feel like cooking, and sometimes I don't. If we could allow ourselves the freedom of doing things when we feel like it and reduce the pressure, we could cut our stress in half. It's great to be super productive, but if you are stressed, snapping at your kids and yelling at people when you are driving, then maybe being kinder to yourself could help. I have found that the nicer I am to me, the more relaxed I become, and I am a hundred times more productive.

As I take my supportive self with me, and drop that mean one, everything I do becomes easier. If something doesn't get done, I don't go into self-attack. I go into self-love, or try to. I begin to look at all the things I did get accomplished and acknowledge what a great job I did today. I remind myself of the bigger picture: my own well-being.

# Why can't I be perfect

Many of my clients get mad and upset with themselves when they have fallen off the diet, haven't exercised enough, or don't have as clean a house as they feel they should. Some are upset because they aren't making enough money. Sometimes they're upset they're staying in a bad relationship or job that makes them unhappy. The list of demands or "should haves" is limitless and we each have different lists. These lists, goals, or rules for living are not wrong. It's the spirit in which we do them and in the thought behind them that either empowers us or stresses us out.

These lists can become something we have to do to "become" valuable or loveable, and if we don't accomplish them we punish ourselves in thought and sometimes in action. We can be cruel and unloving with these unrealistic expectations, these lists of things we must accomplish.

My client Emma, a middle-aged social worker, was telling me that she can't relax or have a good day unless she does yoga. On the days that she doesn't do yoga, she's upset. She's miserable, and mad at herself. The night before, she was so mad at herself that she ate a chocolate bar, which made her hate herself more.

As she talked about this she started to cry, which she usually doesn't do. Through her tears she told me that no matter what she starts, she always fails. She was so sad and disappointed in herself. I listened, and as I listened all her sessions came flooding back to me, all the times she was excited to start something, to practice yoga, to save money. All the goals, and then all the times I watched her coming in dejected, sad, because she failed the new diet, she had missed yoga class, and she continued to struggle with money. She would tell me her failures and look to me anxiously, waiting for me to treat her the same way she treats herself. Sometimes I feel like my clients see therapy as confession. They tell me all the things they are doing wrong and they wait for me to condemn them the same way they do to themselves.

I thought back to all her struggles and the back and forth of her feelings about herself. It's easy to like yourself when you are doing what you think is "good": eating well, being organized, exercising, and being in a good relationship. But when we fail, when we fall off the diet, lose the relationship, make a mistake, we reject ourselves. I thought, my God, what we do to ourselves.

As I was listening, I was inspired to say to her: "Maybe it's time to learn to love you a little more. We have been here so many times, and I feel the lesson for you is to let all of this go and try to forgive and love yourself through this disappointment. Give yourself unconditional love and support and be compassionate. We are not perfect, and to have all our self worth and our feelings depend on the things we do on any given day takes a toll. We make up so many rules and have these rigid ideas about what's important and then we believe them. We create a box with these beliefs, and then put ourselves in it and it gets tighter and tighter in there."

"I know people who are happy and peaceful and don't do yoga," I continued. "You have made this your one way to get to your peace and happiness, and most importantly, your acceptance of you. Practicing yoga and dieting has become your only path to accepting and loving you."

As I was writing about this session, it hit me--I do this with money. I am very anxious about having enough money and this belief of mine locks me in to the same pain, fear, and anxiety box. I tell myself if I only had more money I would be happy! Now, intellectually I know many people who don't have tons of money and are happy. And also many people who have money and are unhappy. Yet I still hold this belief.

In this moment, as I think about this, we heal each other, as often happens between therapist and client. Later, I tell her I think perhaps the gift in all of this, in all the rules that she puts on herself and keeps breaking, is that on any given day she can learn to hold the thought of loving herself more unconditionally. Her belief that "I can't feel relaxed or feel okay about myself unless I do yoga" is such a strong belief, and then it becomes reality.

I gave her an affirmation to try: I love to do yoga when I can, but when I can't I take good care of myself and use other ways to feel peaceful and relaxed.

I could see her relaxing and feeling better, but sensed it was a struggle to let go of this demand, this belief. It's hard to let go of what we think we want. It's hard to choose love over those hurtful beliefs. I told her to just keep saying the affirmation, even if she didn't fully believe it. The affirmation in and of itself brings peace. You will feel better – and then you will see the truth. When yoga becomes just an option, and not a "must," or a "should," then the choice not to practice will lose its power to make you feel bad about yourself.

I felt so sad for her. She looked like a little girl even though she's in her 50s. She was so sad, tired, and disappointed. I tried the best I could to be as loving and unconditional with her as I was telling her to be with herself.

Can you imagine what it might feel like to love yourself with no conditions, just love yourself for who you are and not what you do, look like, or have? Unconditionally?

Emma didn't have to give up on her yoga or the things that are important to her. We all want these things, to be accomplished and proud of ourselves. I just believe when you are more loving to yourself you will get to all of them quicker and with less damage. The things we accomplish can't be more important than who we are and how we treat ourselves. One of the questions I often ask my clients is: What would you say to a friend who told you they were upset about what you are upset about? Would you tell them what you are saying to yourself? That they are lazy, or they never finish anything? That if they don't do it today, all is lost? That they'll never achieve their goals? Or would you be supportive and encouraging? It's always easier to see how badly we are treating ourselves when we realize we would never treat a friend that way. So why do we think it's okay or even helpful to do that to ourselves? I think we just need to practice having this loving relationship with ourselves. We are well worth the effort!!!

# Remember who you are

During my session with Kathy, we got onto the topic of why she is so hard and down on herself. Why does she find it so hard to value her? She couldn't help focusing on the fact that she has no boyfriend, and all her friends are married and now having kids. She has trouble making decisions and picks on herself endlessly, how she looks and her weight.

What I see when I look at her is a beautiful young woman. She is really pretty by anyone's standards. She works as a nurse and is passionate and dedicated with the children she treats. I wonder why she doesn't see herself clearly, and I think how sad for her not to see her beauty now, not to feel her worth. It's all a matter of focus. My clients, and most people, just focus on what they don't like about themselves. Yet the law of attraction states that what we focus on, what we dwell on, is what increases.

I can share with Kathy what I see and challenge her to see from my perspective, but it's always a fight to get people to see their true worth, for them to remember who they truly are. I can tell her I see how caring she is with the kids with whom she works. I remind her that she is a great friend and how much she cares for the people in her life. She is truly a beautiful person inside and out, and every chance I get I tell her that. She is not used to this kind of feedback. We are all so caught up in our "lack" we don't focus on what we do have, and we surely don't appreciate ourselves!

I recently read the book *The Magic* by Rhonda Byrne. It is a wonderful book and I highly recommend it. *The Magic* is about being grateful for what we already have, and how this is the mechanism that brings more abundance to you, because if you are vibrating abundance you attract abundance. The exercises are wonderful and I have recommended this book to all my clients. I like to take it a step further and encourage others (and myself) to look at all the things we could appreciate about ourselves. When we focus on all we are, all our successes, we will bring more into our lives that mirrors back our value and bring us more success!

With Kathy, every chance I get I mirror back all the good I see in her, the truth, and hopefully one day she will be able to take over my job. I recently asked her to make a list of all the things she likes and appreciates about herself and all her successes. She looked at me and said, "I really can't think of any." I was surprised, but then I thought to myself, "Of course she can't think of anything, she spends no time focusing on what's good and valuable about her."

With ease I could rattle off many of her good qualities and accomplishments, because that is my focus. I could sense her reaction. Everything I was saying she wanted to rebut and tell me why it wasn't true. If she was so pretty why didn't she have a boyfriend? If she was so good at her job why couldn't she fix every child she had? What she doesn't see is that if she keeps the focus on not having or not doing, she brings more of that into her life. If she could change her focus and start to see herself as beautiful and lovable, she would bring what she wants to her door. What we focus on increases! I went on with my list of her positive qualities, and told her I wanted her to continue it.

It's up to YOU to change your reaction to yourself. This is not something someone else can do for you.

It's a choice. You can either continue to choose to listen to your inner critic, your ego, or you can choose LOVE. When you start to feel bad, try it. Give yourself a chance. Treat yourself as you would your best friend. Listen to yourself with compassion and try to comfort yourself. Start with your thoughts and then your actions will follow. Accept and love everything about you.

Look at your pets--your dog, your cat, or horse – they are great at self love. They let themselves just be, they don't try and change themselves. They love, they accept, they eat, they sleep, they rest, they play, they take really good care of themselves, and we deserve to do the same.

# Minute by minute

It's a simple choice to choose love versus criticism. We can decide minute by minute, hour by hour, day by day to choose love and friendship toward ourselves. We can look for ways to be more loving and compassionate, to be more accepting of everything that we are, all that we do, and everything we want to become.

I once heard someone say to the man she was going to marry: "You now have my heart, please take good care of it." I thought that's so sweet, but it also reminds me that we have our own hearts to take care of and that's even more important than giving away that responsibility to another. *We have the ability to take care of ourselves like no one else can, if we choose.* We can be the loving god or punishing god to ourselves, the good parent or the bad one, the fairy godmother or the evil stepmother. We could be like Aladdin's genies and grant all our wishes, or we could be Scrooge. If we make these choices more mindfully and choose rightly, our lives will stay on the most beautiful abundant path.

All it really takes is mindfulness and daily practice. It can mean looking for books, affirmations, or spirituality, anything that speaks to your brilliance and empowers you. Anything that doesn't support you or feel good should be put down. You can make a new choice at any given moment or time. If you forget and begin making yourself feel bad, choose again. Look for the right in what you may be making wrong. Look for the good in whatever you are seeing as bad. Forgive yourself or anyone outside of you so that you can freely move back to where you want to be.

# Love is kind

Love is patient, love is kind. It does not envy, it does not boast, it is not proud. It does not dishonor others, it is not self seeking, it is not easily angered, it keeps no record of wrongs. Love does not delight in evil but rejoices with the truth. It always protects, always trusts, always hopes, always perseveres. Love never fails.

Corinthians 13: 4-8

This beautiful verse is often used at wedding ceremonies and it is easy to see why. But what comes to my mind is that this verse could be applied to developing a loving relationship with us.

When we are mindful, we can be patient and kind to ourselves, and we deserve that. Often when we dishonor others it is just another form of self-attack. What we are irritated by in others is what we can't accept in ourselves. Loving yourself is not self-seeking; when you come from this full place everyone becomes included, because it's easy to love others when we feel good. We have so little patience with ourselves, and we keep terrible records of all our wrongdoing. This act is not compassionate or helpful. When we are quick to anger it usually means we need to forgive ourselves and ease up. Nothing that we do can be so horrible to justify self-attack. When we see love, we cast out our judgments of ourselves and any evil thoughts about us.

We can, and we need to, protect ourselves, trust ourselves, and never lose hope in who we are. We can apply this verse to our relationship with ourselves. We can never fail, because love never fails and neither do we. We are a success in who we are and who we become in this world and that has little to do with what we do, it has to do with our state of being.

The next time you hear this verse read at a wedding, think of it in these terms and it will remind you to rethink your relationship with yourself. There is always room for more growth, expansion and love for us.

# Supportive people

When I think about the supportive people in my own life, I think of how kind it is for them to mirror me out of love and help me along my way. It's so rare to feel genuine support from people because they are distracted and too busy being unsupportive to themselves. Some of these people are having a decent relationship with themselves, but many aren't. They are supportive of me, but mean to themselves. Seems like such a contradiction, but we do it all the time. I was supportive and encouraging to my clients long before I was that way to myself.

It took me many years to realize I forgot about myself in helping everyone else. I had to remind myself of this inner forgotten friend that desperately needed my attention. It was as if other people deserved my time and attention, but I didn't? How I came to that conclusion is my own story, and I won't bore you with it, but I can tell you that I don't think or feel that way now.

Therapy is a funny thing. With my clients, I really strived to be the most knowledgeable, loving, encouraging, and supportive person I could be. I hoped that I was creating a new experience for people and that they would feel better, and they did when they were in my office. But when they left, they took their crummy relationship with themselves out the door. I missed the obvious; like the ancient proverb "give a man a fish and you feed him for a day, teach him to fish and he eats for a lifetime," I forgot to teach them how to fish! You get the picture. For them to get a dose of self-acceptance for 45 minutes once a week was not enough for them, or me. So now I teach them what I try to teach myself, and what I am writing to you. Don't miss the obvious in yourself.

Don't give away all your kindness, compassion, and love to others. Give it to yourself first. Then, when you are overflowing you can truly give to others. It is just a new way for us to invest in ourselves.

# Being alone can be fun

I hear people say, "Now that my relationship is over, I am left with just me." They say it like it's a fate worse than death. They look sad and depressed, and the self-loathing is spilling out all over the place. This is the time to be very kind and gentle and to start to learn about yourself – who you are, and what you like. Part of this relationship is getting to truly know what makes you tick. What do you want to do? If you have no "better" distractions, it's a great time to learn to spend some quality time with you. I know you have so little free time– me too – but I can ask myself all kinds of questions during the busiest parts of my day. I can notice me; I can see what I get excited about, and what I enjoy. I can see what depresses me and what makes me happy. I just have to notice me.

We all want to be special, noticed, and valued, and we can be. *We can be the superstars of our own lives.* Why not? There isn't another me anywhere in this world, so this makes YOU and me very special. I am a one-of-a-kind and people pay good money for a one-of-a-kind anything. Value everything that goes on within you. If you do, you can see you are human, not perfect, but special and rare. Scientists say we use only a small portion of our brains and I say we use a very small portion of all that lies within us! We have such power. Learn to grow and nurture your inner resources. Having a very intimate relationship within yourself will grow these resources and give you a more exciting and powerful life. I believe powerful people like Martin Luther King, Jr. and many others were able to do this. They are no different than us, they just tapped into their inner wealth of self and trusted it. So can we.

# The journal remains the same

A few months ago I was looking through an old journal of mine and to my horror realized that as an adult some 30 years later, I am having the same feelings that I did as a teenager. The only difference is the names and places have changed. Well, I thought, that's interesting and a little sad. I was feeling that I was sort of pathetic for being in the same place. But then I tried to talk to myself in a more loving and supportive way. I said to myself, "It's okay. I am sure I am not the only one." Which is true, I see it in my clients, the same core issues over and over. So it made sense. Once it made sense, it became easier to talk to myself in a nicer way. I thought about the notion of having so much power inside and how we are all untapped resources.

Inspirational people *inspire* by the way they talk to you about yourself. They talk about our common experiences in a way that empowers and enlightens you and makes you feel great. These self-help gurus impact us whether it be at their conferences or workshops, or listening to their CDs. Tony Robbins, Wayne Dyer, Jack Canfield, and other inspirational people make me feel good in their presence, and give me hope about me and how I can grow. However, just like my clients in therapy, I take my relationship home with me. I've often thought, well, if I lived with Tony or Wayne, maybe I would be more successful. Or would I argue with him? And keep reminding him of why I can't do any better than what I am doing? In truth, it would probably be a little of both. So, in this new intimate relationship with myself I will commit to talking in a supportive way and encourage myself to stop writing the same things in my journal – put an end to saying the same things over and over. But here's the trick: when I do write the same thing (which I am sure I will), I will love and support myself and not beat myself up!

Here's just a sample of some of my inner rants: "I am tired." "I don't feel like working." "I want my life to be easier." "How did I end up here?" "I am tired." Ugh, I am sick of my own words!

No more! I am giving myself a fresh coat of paint. I am going to encourage myself to try many colors, maybe even change the color every week if I feel like it. What would happen if I could really wake up the resources in me? Could I be a famous therapist like a Carl Rogers and really listen to me? Could I be a great inspirational speaker like a Tony Robbins and encourage myself? Could I be a humanitarian like a Mother Teresa and be loving and forgiving to me?

What would I be doing today if I had this kind of support? The good news is that I do have this kind of support. I can have all of these wonderful role models come alive in me if I can allow it. Since I am not any of these people, my outcome will be different, but it will be mine. My work here may be very different than yours, but that's the fun! What really IS your life's work? What is your masterpiece that you came to create? What did you decide to come to this planet to do? To complain? To lead a boring life? No, to develop the best possible relationship with yourself, so you can know and tap into all your natural resources. Our true natural resources come to us in the most natural of ways. This is when we know we have struck our oil or mined our gold.

# Enjoy who you are

I met with a new client today, Diana. Diana is a very attractive woman in her 50s. As she sat down, I could feel a strong energy from her. She began by telling me her story: she was married twice and divorced both times. She went through the details of these marriages quickly, and she was quite funny and entertaining. As she spoke about her experiences she became more and more animated and funny, and as she sensed my acceptance of her she relaxed and shared more of her story.

In just this brief encounter, with me validating her presence – her strong, funny, and entertaining energy – she caught a glimpse of herself from my perspective. I'm sure people tell her how funny she is all the time, but it always feels good to be appreciated. She went on to tell me about the successful chain of businesses that she owned and operated. I was thinking about how this woman has really encouraged herself in her career, and I wondered what was going on in her relationships.

She described her most recent relationship with her boyfriend Mike, who she found to be emotionally available, and who treated her better than any man she had ever dated. Yet she was ambivalent about the relationship. She didn't understand why she didn't want to stay with this great guy. He was willing to give his time and attention to her, she felt his loyalty and fidelity, and he didn't have any addictions, unlike her ex-husband. He worked very hard as a construction worker seven days a week. Everyone said they made a great couple, and so she had begun questioning what was wrong with her. She asked me what I thought about her not wanting to be with this seemingly great guy. I asked her to tell me more about him, how they had met and how the relationship had started. I knew there had to be plenty of reasons she was having trouble with him, but she did not trust herself.

She said that in the beginning she really liked him and all the attention he was giving her, so that after a few months of dating she started to feel bad about him paying rent when he was with her all the time. She thought she could save both of them money if he moved in with her. I explored how she came to that decision. She explained that at that time her business was going through some difficulty and she wasn't in a great financial place. That made sense to me, she was feeling scared and was looking for support. As she got to know him she realized that although he was kind to her, and everyone said they made a beautiful couple, she found him a bit boring. The last straw came for her when his mother came to stay with them, and he expected her to take care of her and entertain her. She said to me, "I have my own mom, and I do not want another one that I have to take care of." His mom was sick and needed a lot of care. I could tell she felt guilty for saying that. I supported her and told her I could see why it felt unfair and wrong to her, and I noticed she settled back down.

At this point, she had asked him and his mom to move out. It appears that when she was vulnerable and fearful, she made a quick decision to help him financially and herself emotionally. She was scared, alone, and needed support. When her strength came back, she realized it was too quick and she was able to correct the mistake and ask him to move out. She did this when her business was succeeding again, so she had strength to do the right thing for herself.

I could now see part of her story, and as we all often do, she made an important decision under stress and anxiety. My job with Diana was to model what she could do for herself. I validated this rare and unique woman, mirroring her strengths. I supported and accepted her decisions, knowing even if I don't understand why she feels the way she does there is still a story behind it that makes sense of it. My goal is to help her have a better relationship-friendship with herself, so that she can understand her intellect AND her emotions. When she truly understands herself, she will see that when she's stressed she's vulnerable and may want to slow down. She will see her tendency to make decisions for other people that may not best meet her own needs.

Very often, intellectually we know what we should be doing, but our wounds or emotional barriers prevent us from taking those steps. This behavior on our part leads to self-attack. Then we say to ourselves, "How could I be so stupid? What was I thinking?" or "I knew I was making a mistake but did it anyway, what's wrong with me?" This is when we need our own understanding and support the most. I joke with people that our intellectual and our emotional selves rarely meet. The result of that is usually our intellectual self attacks our emotional self. With a real lack of attention and understanding, we deem our feelings as hindrances that just don't make sense.

I would suggest that we introduce our intellectual selves to our emotional selves--and call off the war. I really see that people just don't "get" themselves at all most of the time! So even if you don't understand your feelings, if you can just accept them, you can reassure yourself enough to feel better. I tell people to use whatever reassures them, because feeling better is our goal. Do we really want to keep living out of these wounds? How often are you feeling upset or stressed because you are judging yourself for your feelings?

Back to Diana. Diana told me that she was still seeing Mike after he moved out. She complained that he calls her constantly and texts her. I asked her if she told him to stop, to give her some breathing room, and she looked blankly at me. "Oh, I can't do that," she said. I asked why not, and she said, "I don't know, I just feel bad." I said, "That's okay. We will figure out why you can't tell him what you need." I asked her if she would like to be able to tell him that she needed space. She said, "Yes, but I just can't seem to do it...."

I told her that when we want to change something about us, it helps to make sense of why we are doing it, and then lovingly, we want to encourage ourselves to take the next step. We don't need to beat ourselves up for not being able to make changes; we just need to understand the emotional barrier. Once we do this, the barrier may or may not crumble away. Whatever the outcome, our response can always be the same: love, support, and encouragement for ourselves. Just like you would tell a friend who was struggling with an issue, we can say to ourselves: This is hard for you but don't give up!

I introduced this concept of developing a good relationship with herself. Like many of us, she "knows" it is important. She said, "I know you're right, but I am so busy I don't give myself much time." She told me that anyway she thought she did like herself and treated herself well. She explained that she often went for pedicures and massages. I agreed with her that those things feel good, but that is external pampering. I couldn't agree more that a massage is wonderful, but I am talking about internal pampering.

She laughed, and said, "Yeah, I don't give myself much of that!" I told her that so few of us do. We just aren't taught that, and it's okay.

She then said, "But I am in my 50s, isn't it too late?" I asked her if she felt it was too late to be in a loving relationship. I said, "How do you feel about Mike? You aren't saying it's too late to get involved with him? So, if it isn't too late for him, why would it be too late for you?"

She laughed, and I continued to share my thoughts about this kind of relationship with ourself. I think it's never too late to make a commitment to loving you. Commit to love every breath you take, every thought you think, every feeling you have, every action you take – everything! That's unconditional love, and it is what we long to get from other people.

Diana said, "Well, it sounds good, but I am not sure I can do all of that." I said, "We can try and see how it feels. You can always go back to your old ways."

# Random acts of kindness

One morning I woke up feeling stressed and anxious. I was thinking I need something to help me feel better, but there's no time for exercise or to call a friend. I turned the shower on nice and warm, and imagined the water was showering me with love. As I felt the warm water, I began to feel love showering all around me. I took my soap and suds and imagined washing away all my stress and worries, and I watched them going down the drain. I thought about everything I was beating myself up for and all my overwhelming feelings. I reassured myself and reminded myself that I am doing the best I can. That I can relax, and everything would work out just as it should.

I try to do this when I'm stressed and it really helps me. It's easy and it works. Try a "Shower of Love" the next time you feel stressed. For some people it helps to imagine it is God's love showering down on them. I know sometimes people avoid doing these exercises because they feel silly, but try it and see how you feel!

It seems to me that most of us don't have a great internal support system. We always look to see who's around for outside support, but internal support gets overlooked. It really helps to learn how to self-soothe. When we are anxious or fearful, we tend to self-attack instead of self-soothe. I constantly suggest ways for my clients to reassure themselves. Whatever areas your issues fall onto, you need a lot of reassurance and soothing words for yourself. If you tend to be scared around financial issues, it helps to comfort yourself with reassuring affirmations like, "My income is always increasing from expected and unexpected sources." I love that affirmation from Louise Hay (renowned author and founder of Hay House publishing).

You have to encourage yourself to move out of fear whenever possible, because it just doesn't help us and puts so much stress on our bodies. The goal is always to feel better, so you want to say and do reassuring and soothing things to feel better. Some of my clients pray to God or their angels when frightened. Whatever works for you, use it.

It takes some convincing to see that feeling bad doesn't help any situation. You could be a 100 percent right to feel fearful, but how does staying in these states really help us? It helps to accept our fears, to try to understand them, and gently help ourselves out of them to enjoy our day.

# In my eyes

I once heard a client say about his granddaughter, "She could never do anything wrong in my eyes." What a sweet thing to say! I tell my clients to say that to themselves and work on believing it. "I could never do anything wrong in my eyes." If we could all say this about ourselves, what a difference this simple statement could make. It doesn't mean you don't make mistakes, it just means you look past them to see who you truly are and all the good things you do on a daily basis. Be amazed about you--"Wow, that was nice of me!" or "Look how much I got done today!" or "Look how I let my whole house fall apart, so I could rest and relax. What a good job I did taking care of me!"

Look at all you did right. Don't focus on the two mistakes you made and are now berating yourself about. Those mistakes help you learn and grow. We are not perfect, but we walk around expecting ourselves and others to be.

We need to be better spin-doctors with ourselves! Why? Simply because it helps us to be happy and feel better, and that makes us healthier and more productive people. We all know we are more creative and productive when we are feeling good.

Happiness impacts us in so many positive ways. When we are happy, any task we have to accomplish feels easier. The weight of self-attack makes the same task ten times harder. When I am in a happy mood, I put music on and clean the house. When I am fearful or attacking myself, I don't even think to turn the music on. I believe it is as simple as shifting your attention to yourself and not judge yourself, but rather to learn to treat yourself better. To begin to like yourself, and, ultimately, love and value yourself.

# I hate my job

Sam is a nice looking older man in his late 40s, who, judging by his appearance, takes good care of himself. He always looks put together, even in his causal clothes of matching t-shirt, sneakers, and baseball cap.

He owns a catering company, and because it's a seasonal business, he gets very busy for a few months and then things get slow during the rest of the year.

Sam reported feeling stressed and overwhelmed during the busy season, and hates feeling this way because he is cranky with everyone around him. I started our work by helping him see that indeed his business did have some disadvantages. I shared with him that if those were the circumstances of my business, it would translate into seeing triple the amount of clients for four months of every year. How did he think I would feel working like that? This simple validation helped him to see it is pretty unrealistic for him to expect he wouldn't be crazy during this stressful time. But in his mind, felt he should be handling this stress better. When I reframed it for him, he saw my point and how his expectation of himself was both unfair and unrealistic. I suggested it might be better for him to start by just accepting that this is crazy time. With a different approach, a more understanding approach, I thought it could become less stressful.

I suggested he try to go into the busy season preparing for a chaotic, pressured lifestyle, and maybe be extra nice to himself because of it. To tell himself: I am going to take it slow, one thing at a time, and try to relax into the craziness of it instead of fighting it. When he does it this way, he can get so much more accomplished, and with less wear and tear on himself. I asked if he thought he could try to make the insanity fun. Joke around with people, laugh more, and lighten the day up. He acknowledged that he never thought to try to laugh at it, to move beyond his set way of doing things and thinking things. Of course, most of us operate this way, trying to be in control. We all tend to approach our lives this way, but we don't have to. Anything can be fun; it's how we look at it.

If having a good relationship with ourselves is our priority, we will try many different ways to reach that goal. If we have a different goal in mind, then how we treat ourselves will not enter the picture. Our goals can blind us – I want money, no matter what the cost to me. I want the relationship, even when it doesn't feel right. We lose ourselves in the process of achieving. The reality is, there is nothing wrong with achieving, but we want to try to treat ourselves better during the process, because the process is where we live. Having a loving, peaceful attitude toward ourselves enhances our daily lives more than we could imagine.

The other options are to wait for something good to happen outside of us, or to be unhappy. Neither choice seems great to me. What I want for myself, and for others, is to have a more consistent level of love and happiness in our world. We hear people say it's not the quantity of time we have with others, it's the quality. I couldn't agree more. If most of your time with your kids is spent arguing or being annoyed, we would look for ways to improve the relationship. The same is true of the time we are with ourselves, we have tremendous *quantity* but our quality isn't usually so good! Sometimes we wish we could take a vacation from ourselves, but seeing that we can't, we have to find other ways to improve the quality of time we have.

Can you think of ways you can improve the time you spend with you? I think when we are mindful of the idea that time spent alone can be of better *quality*, we can start to think of strategies to enjoy that time more.

# Running on empty

What happens when our lives feel boring? We may have a lot on our plates, running here, running there. While it isn't terrible, we can still feel tired and a sense of "Is this all there is?" or "Is this really my *life*?"

These are not fun feelings, and we have to take great care that we don't add to our discontent by calling ourselves names, or blaming ourselves for feeling this way. We can choose to infuse ourselves with love and try to visualize a life we would like. Some people say they don't like to do this, because it upsets them to think about what they want and don't have.

But many people have read the *The Secret* and are beginning to understand that the more you can visualize something you want, the greater your chance of actually creating it. We just have so little belief in ourselves that we give up. But if other people can create what they want, we can too. There is no difference, no magic pill or special club you have to belong to. You just have to know what it is you want to create. You have to find your passion.

Some people may call them hobbies. To me, hobby sounds boring, like something you do because you really don't have anything else to do. "Passion" sounds more exciting to me. I have watched people who are looking sad and beaten down just come alive when talking about something they are passionate about. It's like turning on a light switch. Investigating your passions starts to fill your empty gas tank.

# Don't kick yourself when you are down

When I see clients who are in pain, one of the ways that I try to help them is by teaching them how to NOT add to their pain. I know that when I am in a bad place, sometimes time just needs to pass for me to feel a bit better. But I will try to really encourage myself as well. See yourself as having a temperature of 103 and still trying to do all your life tasks. I tell my clients to look at it as if you are physically "sick" when you are in emotional pain.

In the movie *Joe Versus the Volcano*, Meg Ryan says "I feel soul sick." If you feel that way, whatever the reason, it's time to try your new inner language. It's like learning French or Italian. I compare it to learning a new language because you have to first decide you really want to learn it and then commit to practicing it every day. Because our inner chat is so constant and tends to be negative, we need to learn this new language with dedication and commitment.

As with anything new that you are trying to learn, you want to be patient and supportive to yourself. You will begin to feel motivated to use this new language mainly because it just feels so much better. This language is critical to use during your down moods or triggered states. That is when we need our own friendship and support the most; the loving words, the positive affirmations, and the encouragement.

Practice pampering yourself instead of beating yourself up. Try bathing yourself in showers of love and attention. Surround yourself with supportive people, not reflectors of our bad states. Many people surround themselves with people just like their inner critic. Or sometimes we bring those parts out in each other. Look at yourself in the mirror, try to see the real inner you, and ask what you need from yourself. You don't need to criticize how you look, or who you are. How about a little loving support instead?

Don't wait for others to tell you who you are. See for yourself the real "you." It is almost like seeing yourself from another perspective, looking at you from a different angle.

Some people believe our spirit lives inside our bodies while we are here on earth. So visualize a spirit who is nothing but pure love talking to the human you. This spirit self is all loving and all forgiving and knows all your human limitations – and loves you dearly anyway. In your spirit's eyes, you can say or do no wrong. Ask your spirit to write the dialogue of your new language. Your spirit self or guide wants everything you desire for yourself and is willing to help and support you.

We all basically want the same things in abundance: love, health and financial stability. These foundations are the same for us all, but how we can achieve them is very different because we are not carbon copies of each other. The ways we achieve our goals are very varied, which is the root of all the creations in this world. We don't have to be envious of each other because the part we each play reflects our uniqueness.

We all have our own story to create, and I wouldn't want yours and you probably wouldn't want mine. The language we choose for our stories helps to create them. I am working on a Love Story... what are you creating?

# No more put-downs

My client Cindy, a pretty, single mom of two young boys, came in talking about feeling so frustrated with Match.com. She met a few guys who seemed nice, but neither had called her back. I noticed her first jab at herself: "I am just too sensitive to do online dating."

I pointed out to her that I have many clients who have had similar experiences. She said she realized she shouldn't take it personally, but she did. Again she said, "I am just too sensitive." I told her being sensitive is such a special quality and she was right, maybe she did need a break from it because it was becoming too hurtful. I fully supported her sensitivity and decision. But this one jab at herself was not helping her feel any better. I suggested her sensitivity is really a gift that needs to be protected and nurtured, not criticized. Did she think that she might be happier if she could learn to like and accept all these parts of herself? I asked her, wouldn't it be better *if you could accept you?*

"Yes," she told me, "but how can I even begin to do that?"

I said, "We are doing it right now. I am teaching you a new language. A language of love for you, a language few of us ever learn."

She asked, "How do I learn it?"

"As you would any language," I explained. "You wouldn't expect yourself to learn Italian in one day, would you?"

"No," she laughed.

I said, "You would have to learn it and practice it daily if you really wanted to be fluent in it. So today you practice accepting your sensitivity for the real gift that it is."

She said she would try, and added that she had never looked at her sensitivity that way before.

I asked, "Don't we learn better from acceptance rather than a put-down?"

She said, "Yes, I know what you mean. One of my bosses, he's very harsh with me and it doesn't motivate me. Yesterday I was so upset I went home crying. But then I was beating myself up over the fact that I was too sensitive and shouldn't let him get to me that way. I can see how I was not accepting myself or my feelings, just adding more blame."

"So his style of management doesn't work for you. It's too harsh."

"Yes" she agreed.

"But aren't you just like him – with you? Don't you treat YOU the way he does?"

She thought for a moment and said, "I do when I am trying to learn something new. I am pretty tough on me. I have two other bosses and they are much more supportive and I can take their suggestions much easier than his."

I responded, "I think we all do better with the loving, supportive teacher or parent or boss. Those people are standouts in our lives. They bring out the best in us in a very loving way. These are the people we usually felt liked by and we really responded to their encouragement. I think, and hope, most people can remember a few people in their lives that were like this."

"Yes, my friend Jenny is like that with me."

I asked, "In her eyes you could do no wrong?"

"Nope. She has known me since I was 11 and she just loves me so unconditionally. I can do no wrong with her." She smiled warmly.

"I suggest you use her as part of your new language. Use her dialogue when you are upset or blaming yourself. Think: what would Jenny be saying? We need to pool all our resources when changing our attitude toward ourselves."

Cindy went on to describe to me how difficult her one boss is. Recently she had to go talk to him and gave herself a pep talk. She said to herself, "I will not let him make me cry." She said she lasted halfway through the meeting and the tears started. Again, I asked if she could accept this in herself and see it as special, and also give herself credit for making it through half the meeting. She laughed and said, "I guess you're right."

We tend to see our glass half empty. I suggest we see the full side. All the things we are doing right.

I told her, "You made it through half the meeting. That is progress. The more you feel this part of you is okay, then you will have much better control over it. It's like when we dread something in ourselves – we want to hide it so badly that it keeps popping out. When you can accept this part of you and honor it, you won't care so much what he thinks. So whether you cry or not becomes less of an issue."

From there she moved onto another struggle. "The other thing I keep blaming myself over is not being in a relationship. I feel like I need to be in one, and that makes me feel weak. I don't like that. I should be able to be happy on my own, so I don't like seeing myself in this needy way. I asked her where she got this idea or belief that wanting to be in a relationship was a sign of weakness. She wasn't sure. I had a feeling it had to do with her parents. It's always the parents!

I questioned her about them. She said her parents split up when she was 16, that her mom was very unhappy, very critical of everyone, and very blaming.

She's in another relationship now, and she is still the same way.

She said, "I know it's because she doesn't want to be alone, so she's staying with someone because of that. She is just as miserable with him as she was with my dad. That's why I think I got out of my two marriages. I never want to be her. Stuck and miserable in a relationship like her."

So I asked her, "Does she seem weak to you for staying?"

"Yes, she does. If she could be alone, she would probably leave him."

"Do you think this is where your fear of weakness comes from?"

"Yes, that feels right. I never saw that. I really don't want to be alone either, but I can't do what she is doing."

This is what I asked her to consider: You may be completely right about your mom, but do you think maybe this is happy for her? If she is always this way in all her relationships, maybe this is her level of happiness and how she does relationships. You said she was very critical with you growing up. She is probably the same with herself. So, I would say a lot of her unhappiness probably comes from the bad relationship she has with herself. I am sure her partners are not helping, but she may pick people who treat her the way she treats herself – not so great.

She responded: "Yes, he doesn't treat her well, so why does she stay? People often wonder why she stays with him. She's so nice and he's a real jerk!"

I said, "I think the answer to that is because she treats herself INSIDE the way her partner openly treats her on the OUTSIDE. She stays because the internal and external treatment is a match. One person does it out in the open and the other in secret.

"So," I continued, "if we look at this 'weakness' you are afraid of in your mom and you, that might help. Do you really think it's a sign of weakness to be in a relationship? What do you like about being in a relationship?"

"I like having someone there at the end of the day to have dinner with, to laugh with," she answered. "Someone to make plans with, take trips with. I want someone to make me feel safe and settled and secure. I want to feel safe and loved, and I just enjoy their company."

"I don't hear any weakness in what you are describing. It sounds like you like the company, and you like to have someone to lean on and share your life with."

"Yes," she replied.

"That's not weakness. That sounds really nice and what we all want."

"I just wish I didn't feel like I needed a man to make me happy."

"I don't think you do," I said. "I think you are just feeling like you do. You can help yourself to feel loved, safe, and settled without a man. This way, when you meet him it will be because you love him and his company, that's all. You won't need him to settle these feelings for you because you can do that on your own."

"Did your ex-husband help you with those feelings?", I inquired.

"No"

"Did the one before?"

"No."

"It might be a good idea for you to practice this for yourself, since it's not happening with them anyway." We both laughed and she agreed.

"Those scared and unsettled feelings, are they very old?" I asked her. "Do you remember feeling them as a child?"

"I think so. I always felt a little anxious, and it got worse after my parents split up."

"Those feelings are partly old and partly new, meaning they may stem from the past but when we feel anything similar to our past in the now, the past pain is triggered too. It's like our feelings, the wounded ones, build up over time. These wounds have many layers. Every time one is triggered, another layer is added. You have probably had the same feelings triggered over and over throughout your life."

"This is why the need for stability and safety gets so intense, and you feel like you can't soothe it. When you were younger you looked to your parents to help and maybe sometimes they could and sometimes they couldn't. Now you are all grown up and you don't look to your parents to comfort you, but you look to your partner."

I've explained that concept to other clients, too. There is nothing wrong with looking to your partner to fill those needs. Except when they can't do it, or don't understand your feelings. This is when you need YOU the most, the adult part of you, to nurture, soothe, and help those young feelings from childhood. There are so many books on healing your inner child, so we might want to use some of those tools.

We need to just know that when these intense feelings come up, they are usually from the past and they need your love and attention – just like a little girl would if she was feeling scared or unsafe. What could you say to her? You wouldn't yell at her or tell her that her feelings are wrong. You would want to help her understand her feelings and then soothe them until they pass. When you practice doing this for yourself you will see you don't *need* a man in your life. You may still want one, but not for those reasons. As we practice this, we will see it is true through our own experience.

When we feel especially deeply, or the feelings don't seem to fit the situation, it usually means our feelings are touching our childhood wounds. When we feel these feelings, let's decide to nurture and nurse these wounds, not make them worse by judging or attacking ourselves for having them.

As Cindy learned where her feelings were coming from, they made sense to her, and so she could be less harsh with herself. She was also able to see that *she was being critical to her*, the very thing she hated so much when her mom did it. Because she just did it internally, she never realized that she just kept doing to herself those same things – criticizing and blaming – that her mom had done to her. Cindy was surprised because she was so loving and understanding to her children. She didn't realize she never gave herself that same love and understanding.

# Can I love myself more today than I did yesterday

There is ALWAYS room for improvement in this area, and I say that in the nicest way possible! I can ask myself: what did I learn yesterday from how I treated myself, and can I improve on that today? Did I treat myself well? Or was I mean to myself? Did I put myself down? Or did I feed myself good thoughts? Did my actions reflect those thoughts? What feelings did I "live" in the most yesterday?

If our thoughts are kind it often has a domino effect, and our feelings and actions then reflect them.

Our moods, our feelings, just reflect our thoughts. Feelings come from our thoughts and then we act out those feelings. We don't have to feel angry, hurt, and frustrated most of the time. Although someone or something outside of us can trigger negative feelings, it is usually our crappy interpretation of the events that causes the pain. Today on a talk show I heard this put in a really interesting way. The guest on the show said her life coach told her that her feelings are real, they just aren't the truth. That's why when we listen to the story of them, we realize they may have been true years ago but not now. Now they are just an experience from the past living inside us. Even in the past they may have been something we misinterpreted — and this doesn't make us wrong, just wounded. It's a wound we don't deserve to relive over and over.

You have the power within you to create the sunny day, the good feelings, and the laughter. You can and have been affecting yourself for a very long time. We keep thinking it's coming from outside of us. But when we take full responsibility for creating our own sunny days WITHOUT self-recrimination, guess what? We blame less. It's not your fault that I feel bad today AND it's not mine. I have just gotten into thinking and feeling something twisted about myself, and now I want to throw it on you.

It's like playing Ping-Pong: I don't like me--I don't like you, and back and forth and back and forth. This game can sadly go on forever if you don't really understand the rules. But don't let it! You have the intelligence to understand that you are either putting yourself down in some way or you are switching it on to someone else. Let's play a new game: I don't put myself down--I don't put you down. I watch every word that comes out of my mouth about myself and if it isn't something okay about me (forget love at this moment), let's shoot for acceptance. If it's a criticism, let's rethink it.

If our main goal in life was to remain happy we wouldn't let others trigger us, but it doesn't feel so simple. As I discussed earlier, we do get triggered, usually around a bad belief and/or a childhood wound. At these times, often the best we can do is realize that we can try to see this situation differently. But if we can't, our next step is to take special care of ourselves. If your child or a friend were hurt, you would do nice things for them to help them feel better. That's what we can practice with ourselves. Instead we usually blame or chastise ourselves.

We have to re-script the words we use when we talk to ourselves. Calling ourselves stupid or crazy is just not supportive. For a while, we have to constantly monitor what we say to ourselves. I try to be on the lookout for nice things to say to myself all day long. This doesn't give you a big ego, instead it helps you see your true value, which we often miss and discount. I remember hearing a parenting tip: "Catch your kids doing something good and point it out." This should be our mantra too!!

I was with my client Laura, an attorney in her 30s, and she was talking about all the things she does wrong at her job. Yet she continues to get promoted despite all the horrible things she tells me. They seem to like and value her but she doesn't see it. She knows she needs to work on her confidence. I talked with her about what confident people do. They rehearse their successes over and over and they dwell on what they do right, not wrong. I asked her to think about how she might feel if from the minute she walked into work, she complimented herself all day long, instead of criticizing herself. Do you think she might feel more relaxed and actually more productive?

I told her I wanted her to get a journal and every time someone said anything positive about her work she was to write it down. We tend to dismiss compliments; usually we either pretend the person didn't say it or we discount it. However, if it's written down in black and white, it is harder to ignore. I wanted her to feel her own value. Obviously her bosses see her value, and I do too. It's so apparent to me how smart she is and how dedicated. But the fact is she doesn't see it and it makes her constantly devalue herself − which keeps her angry, upset, and unhappy. It is not enough for her boss or me to tell her. She has to start to learn to pay attention to herself in this way, so she can begin to believe it.

We think that it's the big things that people do or say that break us. But in some ways, it's the little things that people say or don't say that hurt us so much. This is the same with our treatment of ourselves. It's all the little things we say to ourselves, all the little disapprovals, that really add up and take a toll.

You can look around your house and pick on all the things you need to get done and give yourself a hard time, or you can look around at all you have done in your home and tell yourself what a great job you are doing. Which will feel better to you? Ask yourself, "What did I do right today?" It just feels better to your heart and soul!

# The little things

When it comes to self-care, we think it's the big things that will make huge improvements in our lives, but I find it's really all the little things that add up to some really big, substantial changes.

While talking with my client Susie, a single mom of three daughters, she was telling me how for the first time she cleaned out her pantry while her kids were home. You may think, so big deal? But for Susie it was. She had a belief that she would say over and over to herself: the only times I can get things done are when my kids are not home. But through working on developing a better relationship with her, and better self-care, she started to question that belief. One day she said to me, "You know what? That doesn't have to be true, and if I do this while the kids are home, then when the kids are with their dad, I can do more fun things – like go out with my friends or get a pedicure."

Being a single mom, she, like me, is always multitasking. Doing everything yourself becomes a way of life. I am constantly reminding her that she has only half the parenting help, and needs to lower her expectations of herself. Many single mothers hold themselves to the same standards as moms who have a husband helping them financially and with the day-to-day household responsibilities. I am always telling her it's okay for her to lean on her parents or friends for help, because she needs the support.

In being mindful of this type of self-care, we can make a conscious effort to make our lives easier, not harder. I said to Susie, "I think in the past you used to beat yourself up, thinking that would motivate you. But the self-attack just makes you feel hopeless and tired, and then there is no chance of getting that pantry done. In this instance, you took a more loving approach and challenged some old beliefs. That enabled you to do something that you have wanted to do out of self care and not out of self-attack – a big difference."

She went on to tell me how she was even able to have a nice conversation with her older daughter while cleaning. She was able to get two for the price of one: quality time with her daughter and a clean pantry. She felt really good about herself and her progress.

I reminded her again that we have to try everything to make our lives easier, not harder, and ask for help every step of the way. It's a loving thing to do for you. I joke that so many women I see are on the Giving Channel. We need to switch to the Receiving Channel. I think women are givers by nature, and that's a beautiful thing. But for the sake of our kids and ourselves, we need to be able to sometimes switch to the Receiving Channel. Then we can give freely, from a full plate, not a broken or cracked plate. It's the little breaks I give myself, like picking up that rotisserie chicken for dinner and letting any guilt over it go, that helps. Look for ways to make your life easier and simpler.

I find that when we give ourselves these little things and take care of ourselves in these little ways, we get a huge payoff. We feel better and have more time to enjoy our lives. Many women and men I see have so much guilt. A big part of self-love is to let that guilt go and ask for help. Focusing on yourself and being mindful allows you to tune in to you, to know what your needs are and how you can best meet those needs. It is not being selfish. It really is just taking better care of you, and then you and all those in your life reap the rewards.

# What have you been rehearsing and projecting

We spend so much time rehearsing our failures. How much time do you spend anticipating all the things you're afraid of, such as what might happen, what might go wrong? We worry and worry about things that for the most part never happen.

We know that worrying is kind of a waste of time, but we find it hard to stop, hard to not think about the worst outcome in many situations.

If we took all our concerns and instead of worrying rehearse the success of these situations, could you imagine how the outcomes might look different? Remember, what we give our attention to grows.

When you are practicing being more loving with yourself--having a better friendship with yourself, even if you are unsuccessful at something you will know there is a soft place to land within yourself. When you no longer beat yourself up or put yourself down, you will be able to see the success--even in the failure. When you love yourself more, you will praise yourself for trying the best you could; you will see the gift in the disappointment. You will praise yourself for simply trying, for so many people never try.

Along with worrying, we spend a lot of our time either complaining about ourselves or other people. This is the material that most counseling sessions are made up of, and these complaints do hold powerful and helpful information. We are mirrors of each other. What you see as wrong in other people is usually what you don't want to see in yourself. I know it's hard to believe that we spend a lot of time projecting our issues onto other people, but it's true.

It recently happened to me. I was having a disagreement with my fiancé over how he manages his life (which is really none of my business anyway!). I felt he was not living his life with any passion. I was basically judging him and putting him down, saying, "How can you live this way? Don't you want to have a job that has more meaning and passion for you? Don't you want to create more? Make more money?"

He was pretty quiet, and didn't say much. I took his silence to mean that he agreed with me. It took me a few days, but as I replayed the argument, I began to realize that I had completely projected my fears about my own life onto him! When I really thought about it, I started to see that, in fact, he was passionate in many areas in his life, from his hobbies to his children. Suddenly I realized that it was ME that was not living the life I wanted. I was living a life that did not have a lot of passion in it. Needless to say I was a little embarrassed when I understood what I had done. I apologized to him and started taking very seriously the fact that I was not living my passion. I was not living the life I wanted, and I needed to correct that as soon as possible. If I hadn't taken the time to sit with my feelings, to listen to their story, I would never have realized that I was projecting onto him my own insecurities and disappointment. I would have continued to think that it was his problem, not mine.

The moral of this story is that by not tuning into and listening to my own feelings, I may have missed this really important information about myself.

We project our feelings onto other people all the time. Sometimes we feel like we're overreacting to situations, but usually that intense reaction is a tip-off, a red flag that has something to do with a part of us that needs our attention. The next time you overreact, or flip out on someone, try to pause and think, could I be projecting some part of myself that needs my attention?

What is your biggest complaint with this person? Have you felt this way before with other people? Is there a theme to it? If we take complete responsibility for our feelings and see they are no one else's fault, we can begin to see how many times we are projecting. Of course, there are times we are really reacting to someone's hurtful behavior, but almost always, underneath, there is a wound for us, a feeling about ourselves.

Why is this important? You will get to know the real you better. And just as importantly see what your next move in your life should be. For me, the message was: Write the book already!!! Create your own life of passion!

There is another reason this information is important. It can help us not take other's reactions so personally when they flip out on us. We can recognize when someone's reaction to us is a projection and has little to do with what we're doing. That helps us to not be defensive and to try to understand. It can help us have compassion for each other.

We often project our good beliefs along with our bad beliefs. The bad beliefs, or our wounds, are more noticeable because they hurt and usually make us very mad. The good ones don't get as much airtime because they don't raise feelings of the same intensity. Our bad beliefs usually hold a wound or two of ours. For me, not living my life of passion also holds the wound of not feeling supported or encouraged to find my passion early on in my life. Feeling alone, passed over, not important – all of this was what my fiancé triggered off in me. Poor guy didn't stand a chance against all of that!

We are all in the same boat. We all basically want the same things in life, and we just create different pictures. We can rest assured, though, that there is space on the wall for each of our pictures. We all are equally special and have unique gifts. But until we recognize them we can be moody, restless, and disappointed. I recognize this in others, and have a great deal of compassion for people because I can clearly see (unless I am in the middle of a projection) that they are struggling in the same way I am.

We all want good health, success, close relationships, love, and acceptance. And we can all have what we want but we have to start with ourselves. When we are moody and flipping out, we need to have compassion first for ourselves and then for others. We are all fighting our own battles.

In *A Course in Miracles* (a self-study curriculum that aims to assist with spiritual transformation), it is said that attacks on yourself or others are just a call for love. If you find you are the one doing the attacking, you need more love. If they are attacking, they need an offering of love. *The Course* says that we are either in love or fear. I think this is a great way to view the people around us and ourselves, too. I believe that we usually attack ourselves first, when we should be looking to give ourselves high levels of tender, loving care daily. When we are attacking someone else, we think we are giving ourselves a break. But often we are just creating more trouble for ourselves. The more you can see what is really going on within you, the more you can forgive yourself and others.

# Reflections in friendships

Friends and family are a reflection of what you feel about yourself.

When I question my clients about the people in their life and how they reflect their good and bad feelings about themselves, I quite often hear the same things. They tell me that they have some friends who reflect the truth about themselves on their good days, and other friends who reflect their bad feelings about themselves on dark days.

We all have those friends who can put us down in the nicest of ways. Some are friends, and some are family members, but they are all around us. It's funny, because I don't hear as much about the people who are good to my clients as I do about the ones who are negative toward them. The supportive friends get much less time in discussions. I make it a point to tell myself and my clients to cherish the good friends. Don't overlook them. Put your energy into those friendships, because you deserve to have what they reflect back to you – and they deserve it too! We can spend a lot of our time trying to figure out why some friends treat us the way they do, but ultimately it is really a waste of our time. We can never know for sure why someone is treating us in a negative way. Usually you can safely say it is coming from their bad feelings about themselves and these bad feelings are being projected onto you. It can feel so personal, but it's not. I simply say to my clients: Happy people don't make you feel bad. They have no need or desire to.

People who are hurt and struggling tend to take it out on everyone around them. I joke and say, "Be glad you are not them." Make a list of your friends, and if you have more unsupportive or negative people in your life than positive, supportive ones, then possibly this is expressing a faulty belief you have about yourself. Don't get caught up in the challenge of trying to get a friend to treat you better. They are either good to you or they are not. Most of the time this pattern doesn't change much.

If the majority of your friends are good to you and supportive, that's great. It means you are probably feeling more of your good feelings and thoughts about yourself than negative ones. If you have equal amounts of both positive and negative friends, it may reflect where you are at and whom you gravitate to at the moment. Maybe on your good days you seek out that loving reflection, and on the bad ones you seek out the other.

I know our beliefs started to form the minute we were born, whether we were told we are not good enough or felt it or inherited it. We also can wrongly perceive negative things from our family or friends. Look at how often we perceive the wrong thing as adults. As adults we can take something very innocent the wrong way.

Can you imagine then how many things we misperceived as children? As a child you take everything personally. I know that being very sensitive myself, I took it personally when my parents had stress. Somehow I felt it was my fault.

Most of us have people in our lives who when we are feeling down will agree with these bad feelings and will support these faulty beliefs. Thoughts like *I am not so great, my relationship isn't that great*, or *my life kind of sucks* run through your mind when you are feeling down. Those people reinforce what we are saying to ourselves and what we believe. In those moments they will agree with you and you might feel understood. However, what you believe may not be true.

We can learn to challenge and look at these beliefs, and say that's not true even when it strongly feels true.

We have other people in our lives who see the best in us. They see how smart and how talented we are. They support us, and seem genuinely invested in us feeling good and staying in a good place. These friends represent the truth about you. These are the friends who when you're feeling down can lift you up – not bring you down. These friends or family members support every idea you have and every new adventure you want to go on. So on any given day, talk to the friend that's super, super supportive, who represents the truth of who you are.

It doesn't mean get rid of the negative people in your life. I don't believe that's the right way to go, especially if they are family. It means remember they are in a hurting place in their own life and can't accurately reflect themselves or you back. I tell my clients we are all evolving souls and we all need love and support. Part of taking good care of us is recognizing that if I am in a bad, vulnerable place, hanging out with my negative or controlling friends is not a good idea. Know where you are at, and then you will know how to best take care of you.

As I discussed earlier, I love inspirational speakers because they speak to your authentic, true self. That's why you feel so good when you listen to them. Entrepreneur, author, and performance strategist Tony Robbins can be like a really good friend. He and others like him focus on who we truly are and all the wonderful things we have inside us, the parts that if nurtured could grow, take shape, and help form beautiful lives. Those are the people who speak to the truth of who we are, and those are the people we should listen to. So, if you don't have a lot of people in your life supporting you, you can seek out books, lectures, workshops, therapists, and life coaches. Seek those people out because they speak the truth about you.

We are all the same and all have so much to offer this world. Many clients feel bad for feeling jealousy toward others. I point out that this feeling is a good feeling not bad even though it can feel bad. Jealousy gives us a clue to what we want. So If I am jealous of a friend who has an exciting career then that feeling tells me I want and can develop that in my own life. This person is showing me what I want and if I can support myself enough I can create the same. Take notice the next time you feel jealous, it's an important clue.

Nobody is better than anybody else. When you understand your value and see your value, you can create from that place what you truly want to create. Look around you: Who is reflecting back to you what you truly want to believe? So many people reflect back so many different things, so choose only the good to take in – and discard the bad. Say to yourself: That's really not me. I'm a good person and I try really hard in life. I'm nice and I'm a good, caring friend and I deserve to have exactly the life that I want and that is special to me.

I tell clients to do what I had to do, and continue to do, so that I don't fall back into old bad beliefs and self-criticism. And that is to flood yourself with the truth and the good about you. I listened to Hay House Radio, where there is nothing but speakers who teach ways to love and support you. I turned off my TV and read many spiritual books that actually felt good and that support the loving God I have come to know. I am constantly watching self-help gurus like Tony Robbins on YouTube to keep me motivated and feeling good. My clients say, I don't have time. I say, you do. And you deserve to do this. I downloaded audio books so I could listen while I did wash and cleaned and cooked. I watched YouTube in between seeing my clients. I made time and so can you – there are ways.

All of this I have done for me, and for you, to fight against this epidemic of teaching ourselves that somehow we are not good enough. Nobody has the right to put you down, and certainly you don't want to put yourself down. You have to feel you deserve the very best treatment from you. You have to keep having the hope to live your dreams no matter what!!

# I found my star

When you can trust and listen to YOU and value YOU, then your next step doesn't feel so high to reach. And even if it does, you will say to yourself (with love and patience), I can do it. So basic, but isn't that the way? Basic, but we just don't do it. We wait and hope either someone else will do it, or by some miracle someone will discover us and make us feel like a star. I say we take the time to discover ourselves!

If we truly nurtured ourselves and everything that lies within us, our true selves, the reason we are here, would become clear. We are powerful, beautiful beings. We see the beauty in nature, yet we are part of this landscape too. Nature is not perfect but we accept its imperfection and see its beauty. We don't say, "Look at that fat, ugly stream" or "Look at that imperfect rose." We appreciate beauty in its natural state. Let's see the beauty in ourselves, and each other, in the same way, since we are all here together. Today, notice the beauty in you and in everyone you come in contact with. People are beautiful – just like the flowers, the trees, the oceans. We just aren't taught to look at each other in wonder and amazement.

There are so many beautiful flowers that we can admire, and do we ever say, "Because this one is beautiful, the others are less so?" Let's feel the same with us. When we fall in love or have a baby, we do it for a short time. We gaze lovingly at each other then. Let's keep those feelings of love and wonderment going. We don't criticize a flower or a bird for being different. How have we learned to do this to ourselves? I don't know, but let us stop now.

# Value the valuable

Wouldn't it be great if every day you saw your true value? You felt your worth? You knew you were walking down your own yellow brick road to a life of meaning, happiness, and abundance?

We are all beautiful like butterflies, but we are walking around feeling and believing we are caterpillars! It's time to look within and discover what you have discounted in yourself. It's easier for us to see the beauty and worth in others, but harder for us to claim it as our own.

But if we can see it in others, it must also be within us or we wouldn't be able to recognize it.

Practice self-discovery daily and try to value everything about yourself. We are so unique, we are our own masterpiece, each one of us individually crafted and specially made. We are born equipped for and prepared for our life purpose. We have wrongly trained ourselves to look too closely at what we don't like, and this has made us soul sick. I believe we can unlearn this habit and replace it with the intention to look for, and see, our own value.

I plead with my clients to try it for five minutes, and see if they don't begin to feel better. Getting stuck in our negative feelings and what we don't have or don't like about ourselves just makes us miserable. I ask both myself and my clients: Does this line of thinking help me at all, or does it just make for one more day of misery?

Set your intention, for what you seek. you will find. Seek for gold, diamonds, and pearls. Why not? We have so much untapped wisdom and creativity just waiting to be discovered. Spend some time alone with your good thoughts; let yourself become what you already are.

We are that unwritten masterpiece, that beautiful song that hasn't been sung yet. The block of clay waiting, the unfinished poem, the next great play. Who is to do all these things but us? Whenever I suggest this, I can already hear the "buts" – yet wherever there is a "but" there is someone who overcame it, and you can too. No matter what your doubts, you can still give yourself the gift of letting yourself become fully and freely YOU; that is our purpose.

# Living the high life

Don't you have some days when you just feel great? Sometimes it's because you bought something special or you got that raise, or maybe you just woke up feeling that way.

The feeling usually continues and you feel immune to letting anything trigger you out of these feelings. Things that would normally bother you have little effect. The day goes great, and the world seems to be filled with happy people.

These are the states of mind we can choose to be in more often that would draw our best life to us. On the days I am feeling good, writing is a breeze. On the days I'm triggered into feeling upset and hurt, writing is not a good idea, and it's usually on those days I decide writing a book is a waste of time. It takes loving yourself, and understanding that when you are down it is temporary. So, don't trash your dreams during those times. Just wait until you're in a better feeling place to make any decisions. The worst time for us to make any decisions is in those triggered states, because we are not our own best advocates in those moments. We say and do things we regret.

For myself, I have learned that when I am in a bad way I need to give myself a time-out from anyone I like, so I don't hurt him or her. I try to be at least civil to myself, but during those moments it can be challenging to be self-loving. I can still try to treat myself nicely. When you are mad or upset at your friends or your kids, you always try to still treat them nicely. Don't we owe that much to ourselves as well? Don't overlook this inner friendship.

My client Tommy, a musician and college student, always wants to break up with his girlfriend when he's in a bad place. He comes in and talks about feeling discouraged in his life and then it moves to his relationship. At this point, he concludes the relationship doesn't meet his needs and he should end it. Now last week he was just saying how much fun he has with his girlfriend. I try to urge Tommy to wait a few days until he's feeling better to make any decision about the relationship.

"You feel bad now," I said to him during one such session, "but if you break up with her you will probably feel worse."

The following week he came in and declared, "Wow, I was in such a bad place. I can't believe I was actually going to break up with Michele."

Once he was out of those feelings, and not projecting them onto his girlfriend, he could see things much more clearly.

Being disappointed in you is probably one of the toughest feelings not to act out on. It's in these moments that we need support from our friends – and ourselves – the most. It is in the moments when we think our life sucks and it isn't getting any better that we most need to have some positive regard for ourselves. We have to remember it's temporary and we will feel better and pick up our lives again. In these moments, we need every tool we've learned: our best affirmations and our most loving and non-judgmental thoughts. The problem I see is that many people don't feel like doing anything that may take them out of these feelings. Often they are so self-blaming they don't think they deserve to feel better.

I say to them: "Just try and give yourself some TLC, and only be around people who will do the same for you. If you have to eat ice cream, it's okay. Just try and be accepting and these feelings will pass." When they pass, the sun is shining again and we are back to growing and creating. We need a little rain to appreciate the sunshine. Don't fall into the trap of thinking the rain will never stop, it always does. So get your best umbrella out and take good care of you until your sun is shining again.

We are all so special, so unique, so creative, and smart. We have to learn to see and value these wonderful truths about ourselves. The more we can see them the more brightly our sun shines.

# Delete delete... insert

I have noticed in myself, and in many of my clients, that we get stuck in patterns of thought. Like on an old record player, the needle gets stuck in a groove. Without even realizing it, we think the same kinds of thoughts all day long, which affect our emotional state for the day. These repetitive thoughts can cause low levels of anxiety or sadness.

It's funny how until you try to think different and more positive thoughts, you don't even realize how stuck your thoughts are. I always viewed myself as an optimistic, positive person, and I would deny that this could be going on inside of me. But when I started seriously working with affirmations and re-scripting, I could see how stuck my thoughts had become. I noticed I would have good weeks where the affirmations were easy to say and I felt better, and then I noticed on some days they made little difference and I was back to my old feeling state.

I joke with my clients that it's like we have a default setting that brings us right back to our old thoughts/beliefs about ourselves, and we end up feeling those same old feelings. During those times it's more of a challenge to like myself and take good care of myself. These are the times when exercising and eating right become harder, and all my bad beliefs about myself come flooding back. Sometimes it feels like all I can do is hold on and not get washed away by them. It amazes me to think I had no idea that any of this was happening!

My remedy has been to rewrite and try to insert not only more loving self-talk, but new phrases, called affirmations, to say over and over until I pull myself out of that rut. I literally have to try to delete and rewrite my thoughts.

When I realized how many of my clients were stuck in similar patterns, I began to point it out to them. They began asking me, how can I begin to think differently, what can I use to replace my negative thoughts? I give my clients some of the following affirmations to say when they notice they are starting feel down, anxious, or sad:

I love myself.

I am easy with myself.

I can do no wrong.

Nothing is more important than how I feel.

I support myself.

I support my dreams and desires, it's never too late and I have just begun.

I am beautiful inside and out, and I love me.

I will not let what other people do upset me.

I do not need anyone to do anything for me to feel happy, at peace and safe.

I will not put myself down, criticize myself or other people.

I will move my body so my thoughts will slow down.

I no longer believe these thoughts, they are just habits and they are not true about me.

I recall all the nice things people say about me and I think about them.

I have a right to feel happy and at peace with me.

It's easy to let go of beliefs that hurt me.

These are just a few. There are many affirmations you can find online and in books that might fit you better. It's important when using affirmations that they fit you, feel right, and are believable to you. If you say an affirmation that is really too far off from your reality, it's only going to frustrate you. My clients tend to like the ones I give them because I know them and the areas around which they have wounds. So you may need to go on a hunt for some or work with a therapist or life coach to help you personalize them for yourself. It's really worth the time and effort. It may feel a little like brainwashing, but after a while you will notice your beliefs changing. When they change, your life naturally expands and you get more of what you want.

The goal is to feel better and create new beliefs. You already know the old ones are not helping, and even if you don't believe the new ones just yet, they usually feel better than the old ones. Just as we want the people we love to feel better when they are down, we need to do the same for ourselves. It just takes some mindfulness and remembering when to use them. If someone has upset you or something goes wrong in your life outside of you, that's not necessarily the time to use them. In those moments, you need to listen to your feelings and help yourself through them with love, support, and acceptance. Then you can get to affirmations.

Affirmations are best used to create new beliefs when not too much is going on. Use them in your day-to-day life when you don't feel at your best and you don't know why. This is the silent attack and you can fight back with easy, new, scripted thoughts. Rewrite, re-script, and insert new healthy story lines. Practice, practice, practice deleting those thoughts that are silently getting you down or making you anxious; you are worth this fight.

# One Day

I want you to take the One Day challenge. For *one day*, decide to be nice to you. Make yourself a priority and don't let yourself think anything negative – not once for the whole day. If you do, just say "delete" and replace it with a nicer, more supportive thought. It's fun to try and it makes you see just how hard you can be on yourself. When you do this, you will notice that you feel better. We don't realize how draining negative words are and how much they actually weigh us down. Words really affect us. Depressing words drain you and empowering words bring you alive. Try it. Say something negative and see how you feel. Then say a positive statement. Isn't there is a big difference?

# Yes Day

Now that you have had some practice in developing a more loving relationship/friendship with you, it's time to change things a bit.

Stop saying "no" and start being nice. Say "yes"! Have you seen the movie *The Yes Man* with Jim Carey? In the movie, a simple decision on his part changed his whole life for the better. It was the decision to stop saying no and only say yes. Of course, it got him in a lot of trouble too, but the idea behind it is that we say no to ourselves so often out of fear. What would open up for us if we said yes instead? Well, a lot of crazy stuff happens to him, but he also grows as a person. If you haven't seen it, rent the movie. It's very funny.

We can be so mean to ourselves. We say no to our dreams, we say no to our feelings, we say no so often to what we want. We need to learn to spoil ourselves. And spoiling ourselves can be a good thing; it actually doesn't make you rotten. I spoil my children all the time and it's made them happy kids. They know and they trust that I have their best interest and their happiness as my priority. They know I'm happy when they're happy, and I do my best to make them happy. But honestly, I couldn't do that if I wasn't treating myself better.

My relationship with myself and making myself happy has to be a top priority. It starts with me and what I need, whether it is going for a massage, going for a walk, hanging out with my friends, writing, or just having a glass of wine. All these little things make me happy.

This is all part of having a loving relationship with yourself, and it will directly impact your level of abundance in every relationship you have, your career, and even your health.

Try some of these affirmations:

It's easy for me to say yes to my dreams, my life, and who I truly am.

I say yes to treating myself kindly and looking at what I am doing right.

I say yes to my strengths and feel proud of every single accomplishment.

I say yes and accept every feeling I have, every fear, doubt, and insecurity.

I say yes to supporting my feelings and understanding them when nobody else can.

I say yes to learning what it means to truly, unconditionally love myself.

I say yes to giving myself everything I so easily give to others.

I say yes to listening to me, to being mindful of me, and to being supportive, kind, loving, and gentle.

I say yes to creating the best possible friendship with me.

Say yes to you more often. It's a good habit to get into.

# The Golden Compass

Wouldn't it be great if we were born with a built-in compass? If we always knew what direction we should be going in? Well, if we sit still for a few moments and listen, our internal compass will point the way. It works as if you were holding an actual compass, which, when you hold still for a moment points North, South, East or West.

We all have within us the ability to know exactly what we want in our lives and how to go about it. It can get confusing at times, though, because life pulls us every which way. Some things pull us or grab our attention so much that we feel we don't know which way is up or which way is down.

This is when we need our compass the most – and it is usually the last thing we do. We may at these difficult times seek out advice from friends, family, books, or even have wine or anything else that may aid us. What we forget is that we are already well equipped to figure out our feelings, our lives, and ourselves, if we can just give ourselves some time alone.

I believe we were each given a Golden Compass at birth. Take yours and hold it in your hand. Be still for just a moment, and let it point the way. The only thing you need to do is give yourself the time to use it.

I know, time, time, time… who has time, you wonder. We do! We reflect and meditate all the time, so this is an easy, no pressure task. Think about the things you already do that are meditative. Driving is meditative, so is listening to music, taking a shower, zoning out, daydreaming, or just the traditional sitting quietly. It doesn't matter how you are sitting or what waterfall you are under or if a candle is burning. What matters is that you give your attention to you when you feel lost or you have been treating yourself unkindly. Give yourself a second: check in, FEEL, and ask for help and guidance.

Some people would call this Golden Compass God. Others would call it your inner voice or intuition. Choose the label that has meaning for you, but choose it and try to use it. That is something no one has the ability to do for you. This special compass keeps us heading in the direction that is truly ours and no one else's.

Sit and ask yourself: In what direction are you headed? Are you off track? Are you following close to your path? What point of the four directions are you following? If you are lost and don't have any direction, set your compass to L for the destination of Loving yourself. Follow the L. Are you staying with good supportive thoughts or are you veering off to S sadness or A anger or N neglect? If you can keep the compass set to love, self care, and compassion, then you can find your way much more easily. It's hard to find your place in this world when you are stuck in anger, depression, anxiety; you just get further lost. When you are filled with self love and self care, direction is easy and you find where you need to go every time.

The other day I was feeling confused, not sure where to go with this book or if I should even continue. I was letting my mind pull me off my path with sadness and doubt. I went downstairs in my office and meditated for a short while, and I saw a Golden Compass. I knew it had to do with how I was feeling: directionless and lost. I was reminded that I was neither, and had all the tools with me to help me get back on track.

If I remember my destination, which is treating myself better today than yesterday, then no matter what I do, whether it's writing or going out to dinner with my family or working, I will always know my direction. I just have to have enough mindfulness to remember to give myself a moment of my time to sit, be still, ask, and then listen to the wisdom we all have within. Then this Golden Compass will be glowing with self love and will point us in the direction that feels right every time.

# Children Learn What They Live

By Dorothy Law Nolte

If a child lives with criticism, he learns to condemn...

If a child lives with hostility, he learns to fight...

If a child lives with fear, he learns to be apprehensive...

If a child lives with pity, he learns to feel sorry for himself...

If a child lives with ridicule, he learns to be shy...

If a child lives with jealousy, he learns to feel guilt...

BUT

If a child lives with tolerance, he learns to be patient...

If a child lives with encouragement, he learns to be confident...

If a child lives with praise, he learns to be appreciative...

If a child lives with acceptance, he learns to love...

If a child lives with honesty, he learns what truth is...

If a child lives with fairness, he learns justice...

If a child lives with security, he learns to have faith in himself and those about him...

If a child lives with friendliness, he learns the world is a nice place in which to live.

This is a very powerful poem, and I remember reading it years ago and thinking HOW true. It's a poem of mindfulness. Be mindful how you are with your children. It impacts them in ways we don't realize. Children are living what they learn and so are we. We have to ask ourselves as adults what we have learned, and if it doesn't sound like the second verse, it's not too late. We can take control and create a beautiful environment within us. Take a look to see how you are living in your inner home. How do you talk and relate to yourself? You can either continue to create the first verse, or you can begin your work on the second. I prefer the second, how about you?

I know writing this book and working with my clients has kept me on the path of mindfulness within my own relationship with myself. I have seen that at times I am challenged with myself to keep treating myself better and better. Some days it comes very easy to like and feel good about myself, and other days I have to go back to the basics and just do for me what I would do for anyone else in my life.

I can see that my relationship-friendship with myself has grown and deepened. I have taken the challenge to love myself more every day and I am determined to stay on this path. This path has given me the confidence and the support I needed to even write this book. I have written my entire life and have thrown out just about everything. The environment I was living in didn't support my dreams, my intelligence, or my creativity. That has since drastically changed. I have called off the war and called a cease-fire. Why? There have been many positive side effects in my relationships and my work now, but the main reason is that I just feel so much better now then I ever have! I say to my clients all the time, don't you want to feel better? This is the path to true happiness, and I hope you challenge yourself and stick with YOU. You are so worth it! We need the real you to step forward to be happy, to create, and just have fun.

I wish you all the best in creating this beautiful relationship-friendship. Don't let yourself be the forgotten friend.

Dear God,

Please help me to love myself,
Please help me to forgive myself,
Please help me to have more compassion for myself,
Please help me to have more patience for myself,
Please help me to trust you and my own inner wisdom,
Please help me to listen to myself,
Please help me to see myself clearly,
Please help me to be grateful for everything about me,
Please help me take loving actions,
Please help me to let go of all fear and live in your love,
for there I am forever safe.

Amen

# A List of Self-Love Tools

## *Books*

***The Eagle and the Rose,*** Rosemary Altea

***Illusions,*** Richard Bach

***The Magic, The Power, The Secret,*** Rhonda Byrne

***Angels in My Hair,*** Lorna Byrne

***Chicken Soup for the Soul,*** Jack Canfield

***The Power of Intention,*** Wayne Dyer

***The 7 Day Diet,*** Emmet Fox

***The Meaning of Life,*** Viktor Frankel

***The Art of Loving,*** Erich Fromm

***Beyond the Self,*** Thich Nhat Hanh

***Heart Thoughts, How To Heal Your Life,*** Louise Hay

***Getting the Love You,*** Want Harville Hendrix

***The Astonishing Power of Emotions,*** Esther and Jerry Hicks

***Modern Man In Search of a Soul,*** C.G. Jung

***Glynis Has Your Number,*** Glynis McCants

***Believe in Yourself,*** Joseph Murphy

*Gestalt Therapy Verbatim,* Frederick S. Pearls, MD PHD

*The Intuitive Way,* Penny Pierce

*Seth Speaks,* Jane Roberts

*Client Centered Therapy, On Becoming a Person,* Carl Rogers

*How to Play the Game of Life and Win, Your Word is Your Wand,* Florence Shovel Shinn

*Vibrations,* Kevin Todeschi

*Healing Grief,* James Van Praagh

*Angel Therapy,* Doreen Virtue

*Conversations with God,* Neale Donald Walsch

*The Science of Getting Rich,* Wallace Wattles

*Many Lives, Many Masters,* Brian Weiss

*The Quickening, Affirmations,* Stewart Wilde

*A Return to Love,* Marianne Williamson

## YouTube Videos

Tony Robbins

Jack Canfield

# Appendix

## *Heaven's gate: A meditation*

Here's a guided meditation that I felt inspired to write and I wanted to share it with you! Just tape it with your iPhone in your voice, which makes the meditation even more powerful. Take a moment to go on this spiritual journey, and see you through the eyes of love-god-source.

Let's take a walk to heaven in your mind. We walk together in a gentle, peaceful way. I am with you, as well as anyone else you might like to invite along, God, your guardian angel, a family member, a special pet, anyone who comes to mind, who puts you at ease... makes you feel safe...secure...and protected as we travel.

We now walk together with our companions by our side, and you will begin to feel the warmth of the sun shining down on your face. With every step you take, you feel the sun's golden rays on each part of your body from your face... to your neck... your chest... your stomach... legs...and your feet. The warmth of this sun seeps into every cell of your body, relaxing it. This special sun has magical properties that heal any physical pain your body may have, or any emotional pain you may be dealing with. Let the sun's rays absorb any burdens, worries, or pain.

With each step you take, you go deeper into this relaxed state of healing. Now I want you to look over to your right and see the path we are approaching... It is nestled in the most beautiful place you can imagine. There are warm streams and bustling wildlife around you. The scents of lavender and roses hit you immediately...you don't even have to be close to the flowers to smell them. You notice the colors of these flowers... they are the most vivid blues, purples, and reds that you have ever seen. They come alive in their vibrancy. The sounds you hear, you can also feel. They are the most beautiful sounds you have ever heard. The running of water, the birds singing... .You can actually feel the sounds running through your body.

We finally come to the end of the path, to an old ornate gate, and you see a heavy chain and lock on it. It's the gate to your heaven. Look at the lock, it looks strong and heavy. The chain that wraps around the gate, and keeps it closed, has many links on it. Each link symbolizes a belief you hold about yourself, and the heavy lock holds the limits you have placed on your life.

Look away for a moment and then look back at the lock. The chain has disappeared right before your eyes, as well as the beliefs and limitations you hold. They are self-imposed and have little meaning. The gate is now free to open to your heaven.

We walk in, and you see all your dreams and your wishes. Everything you ever wanted to become, everything you ever wanted to have, and everything you ever wanted to do or see, is here. Look around for a moment and take this all in.

As we continue, we come across two mirrors, one filled with cracks and chips, and one standing beautiful and tall and flawless.

Stand before the cracked mirror. This is the mirror and the refection you have created. Each crack represents your thoughts about yourself, every attack, every criticism. Every time you treat yourself in an unkind way, a crack appears. This mirror is so marred with cracks; you can no longer see your reflection. All you see are the cracks reflecting back.

Now, come look into God's mirror. Do you see any cracks? There are none. Look at your refection in this mirror. You can see yourself reflecting brightly. This mirror is flawless, and so are you. You can see your spirit – your true self. You see your beauty, the real you.

You can't hide yourself, your soul, your spirit, in this mirror. This is your true reflection, not the cracked one you created.

Take a minute and just look. You can ask yourself, your spirit, any questions about your life, and see and speak to the real you. What do you need to hear? See? Feel? Spend a few minutes with your accurate reflection. Let God show you and tell you the truth about you, no matter how beautiful it is.

It's time to leave, but you are leaving without your burdens and without your faulty beliefs. With each step, you are filled with renewed joy for the path you will create for yourself.

Take your heaven with you, and leave all your limitations at the gate. They have already disappeared.

Open your eyes, feeling alive...feeling lighter... brighter... healed and free. Take with you...your true reflection.

# Janice Fuchs: A Short Biography

Janice Fuchs is a licensed clinical social worker from Long Island, New York, with a Master's degree from Stony Brook University. She has spent the last 25 years providing psychotherapy to adults, children, teens, families, and couples around issues ranging from depression and anxiety to eating disorders and addictions.

After many years of working to help people, Janice has seen that so many struggles come from an inability to clearly understand self-needs and feelings, and confusion over how to take care of self and still maintain healthy relationships and careers. In therapy sessions, she provides a supportive, non-judgmental environment for people to discover what they want and how to work on their self-image, communication skills, and self talk.

In the last several years, Janice began to explore a wide range of spiritual and alternative methods to enhance both her own life and her practice. Those explorations led to this book. Along the way, she realized that the biggest block to peace and contentment stems from not giving enough attention to the relationship with self.

Janice uses the concepts and techniques discussed in her book in her practice today. Though clients make changes in different ways and at different times, she believes her methods can help anyone at any time. Her goal is for more people to develop a loving relationship within themselves, which can translate to an amazing life.

Janice is a mother of two teenage daughters – and two crazy dogs. She does her best to live what she teaches in the midst of the insanity that is life...

www.ingramcontent.com/pod-product-compliance
Lightning Source LLC
Chambersburg PA
CBHW060939040426
42445CB00011B/935